T0392190

All change can be hard, but the birth of a child, while a joyful time, can also provoke worry about every "what if" scenario for a parent. While not everything in life is predictable, writer, and martial artist Brick aims to help families alleviate some of the pressure with this comprehensive guide to achievable methods for lessening some of the biggest safety concerns. Safe and efficient use of a fire extinguisher can contain a kitchen fire before it becomes a conflagration. When it comes to driving, a sober and attentive mindset is key. Sometimes a simple conversation can help, such as with your child's school principal about bullying or with children themselves in stressing the responsibilities and perils of using the internet. Overall, this is a vital and informative guide to safeguarding family by understanding potential threats and remaining aware rather than obsessed. Brick's valuable suggestions prove that when it comes to family safety, the best offense is a good defense.

—Booklist

Praise for *Safest Family on the Block*

Jason writes with humor and a heavy dose of realism, making his tips entertaining to read and practical to apply. Rather than using sensational scare tactics, he empowers readers with specific ideas for increasing safety. With tips for situations from traveling to internet safety, you'll walk away with ideas for keeping your family safe, as well as interesting conversation topics for your next family dinner or get-together with friends.

—**Marielle Melling,** parenting coach, author of *Peace Amidst the Mayhem* and *The BUT Book*

Jason Brick has an uncommon ability to ask the right questions. Too many self-defense instructors believe that the fight is the thing. Trust me, if it gets to the fight, you are way behind the curve. Jason assembled a group of experts and asked them variations on the right question: How do I (or the people I love) stay out of trouble in the first place? This is a book on how to be safe, an order of magnitude more useful and applicable than just another book on how to be an imaginary bad ass.

—**Rory Miller,** author of *Meditations on Violence, Facing Violence* and others

Jason Brick has written an outstanding book packed with invaluable information for parents, caregivers, teachers, and anyone dedicated to keeping their family safe in every aspect of life. I highly recommend this book as an essential resource to help protect and care for your loved ones.

—**Dianne Maroney,** RN, MSN, executive director of The Imagine Project, Inc., and author of *Your Premature Baby and Child, The Imagine Project: Stories of Courage, Hope, and Love* (series)

In *Safest Family on the Block*, Jason Brick has taken the best elements of his podcast and transformed them into the go-to-guide for anyone wanting to improve their family's safety. From teens to technology, this book covers every conceivable aspect of family and gives readers the tools they need to come up with a solid security plan of their own. I'm glad I read this book, and I'm sure you will be too.

—**Gary Quesenberry,** Federal Air Marshal, Ret., author of *Homecoming: A Case Younger Thriller* and *Spotting Danger Before It Spots You* (series)

From playgrounds to passwords, *Safest Family on the Block* is the ultimate survival guide every modern family needs to keep loved ones secure—at home, online, and beyond.

—**Maria Kristina Hayden,** award-winning cyber resilience expert, former intelligence officer, CEO and founder of OUTFOXM, CISM (cyber certification), MSc. (Master of Science in Technology Intelligence, aka MSTI)

In a world where the speed of information changes rapidly, Jason's book is a great compilation of real-world tips on personal safety that is grounded in solid advice. I appreciate his honest assessment of traditional personal safety knowledge with the reality that every family is going to have their own unique perspective of social mores. What might work for one family might not necessarily work for another. That's where his approach to giving the foundational skills to build a safety plan is key. Anyone can take the information in this book and start the conversation on what having a safety plan in place means for their family. The key is to start. Jason's book is the guide we all need to make the first step a little less intimidating.

> —**Kelly Sayre,** founder and president of The Diamond Arrow Group, author of *Sharp Women*

It's one thing to think about safety for yourself, but it's another to think about safety for the whole family. As a parent, you'll be asking yourself questions about everything from how to handle playdates to school. Jason tackles some of the biggest questions parents have through his easy-to-read book with tips and habits to help protect yourself and the family.

> —**Cathy Pedrayes,** safety influencer and author of *The Mom Friend Guide to Everyday Safety and Security*

Safest Family on the Block is a game-changer for family safety. Jason Brick combines his expertise in martial arts, personal security, and parenting to provide a holistic guide that goes beyond typical safety advice. His savvy and know-how comes through in every chapter, making complex security strategies easy to understand and implement. The book addresses everything from home security, emergency preparedness, and cyber safety to dealing with everyday threats that many parents overlook. Jason's approach is clear, comprehensive, and most importantly, realistic—acknowledging the real-world challenges while offering solutions that anyone can implement.

What sets *Safest Family on the Block* apart is Jason's ability to balance the real-world seriousness of security with an empowering, positive message—one that builds confidence rather than anxiety. His advice encourages proactive measures that integrate seamlessly into everyday life, teaching families to take control of their safety in a way that is not just effective, but sustainable.

Every family, whether they've thought about safety or not, will benefit from Jason's expertise. *Safest Family on the Block* is a book that deserves a permanent place on every family's bookshelf. Highly recommend!

> —**Dr. Mary Beth Janke,** former United States Secret Service agent, author of *The Protector: A Woman's Journey from the Secret Service to Guarding VIPs, Working in Some of the World's Most Dangerous Places,* and the TEDx speaker on, "How to Live a Badass Life at Any Age"

Jason Brick has been working for years to educate and support families with practical strategies to help them stay safe. As a person who works with domestic minor sex trafficking victims, having this type of education is vital. Everyone should read this book!

—**Shelley Repp,** CEO, New Mexico Dream Center of
  Albuquerque

If you ask people if keeping their family safe is important, most will say, "Of course!" But if you ask what steps they're taking to ensure their family's safety, many wouldn't have clear answers. That's where *Safest Family on the Block* comes in. Implementing these strategies will keep your family safer.

Jason Brick has compiled 101 practical tips, tricks, hacks, and habits to help protect your family, and I was honored to contribute to this valuable resource. Jason's passion for helping people stay safe mirrors my own, and his book is packed with actionable strategies to make your family's safety a priority.

I highly recommend reading this book, learning from it, and most importantly, applying its lessons. The world has its risks, but it also offers incredible experiences. By implementing the strategies in *Safest Family on the Block*, you can navigate life's challenges and enjoy all it has to offer safely.

—**Alain Burrese,** author of numerous books and videos on
  self-defense, trainer, 5th dan hapkido, former Army sniper

Jason outdid himself on this book! *Safest Family on the Block* is not only a self-defense book as we know it but an overall safety book that covers almost everything we do in our daily lives that should involve being safe. Jason covers everything from self-defense to being aware with an eye toward crime prevention. He even brings in some experts. There is something in this book for everyone. Get the book, read it, and learn from one of the best!

—**John Riddle,** law enforcement officer (RET), combatives and
  firearms instructor, author of *Defend the Now: A Blueprint for
  Safety in Today's Uncertain World*

The types of emergencies you're likely to face will depend in large part on where you live, from earthquakes to wildfires, blizzards, hurricanes, floods, and tornadoes. Events that might bring power outages, interrupted communications and logistics, and medical emergencies. These are the sorts of events that are out of our control, but what we can control is how we prepare for them and respond to them. *Safest Family on the Block* will help.

—**Erika Friday,** founder of Ready Set Moms

I am a mental health clinician and a father, and I highly recommend reading *Safest Family on the Block* by Jason Brick. This book is, quite frankly, that one resource for parents to have that spotlights how to create a family environment that may be considered very safe and resilient. Jason's approach is mainly not just about introducing physical safety measures but even more importantly, building the mental and emotional resilience so needed to navigate the modern world. The practical strategies he provides are easy to implement, based on sound research, and homed in on real-life situations parents encounter every day.

I am a clinician, and I appreciate how this book approaches safety as a multifaceted concept, taking into consideration how the very essence of safety in chilren's immediate environment may affect their sense of well-being psychologically. Jason knows well that children need not only physical safety but, even more so, a sense of emotional security to breed confidence and strength in a child while growing up. His insights ring so true with the therapeutic approaches that I use: helping families create safe, nurturing spaces to foster emotional and mental health.

This book has, personally, been quite invaluable to me as a father. I feel much more certain that I would be in an ever-improved place to deal with, time and again, any such scenario—be it teaching my kids about personal safety, drawing healthy boundaries, or knowing exactly how to respond to emergencies without panic. Jason empowers me through his insights—proactive, rather than reactive—to create an atmosphere of confidence in my ability to protect and care for my family.

—**Jewell Young,** mental health clinician, author and podcast host on World Podcast Network, PodMatch Network, top-50 parenting podcast on GoodPods

There's something in here about almost any danger you can think of. It's fun to read, it's difficult to put down. It's quick, clear, and actionable. This is the book you buy for new parents. Nobody you know should suffer from any of the problems you can so easily find remedies to in this book. I wish I had this book when I was in my twenties and when I gave birth to my son. It's surprisingly difficult to get this information in one place.

—**Teja VanWicklen,** writer/author of *Reimagining Women's Self-Defense: Protective Offense*

I am so proud of Jason and all the hard work he has put into educating families and others on what it truly means to provide safety and security in today's world. I had the pleasure of speaking with Jason on my podcast *Parent Tell* in 2022 about the more subtle ways we as parents can keep our children safe, and that conversation still sticks with me more than two years later. Jason's passion for situational awareness and the positive impact it can have on our families as we navigate our everyday lives is evident in every conversation I've had with him, and this book is further proof. As a parent and former early childhood educator, knowing best practices for keeping young ones safe is something I take very seriously. Jason's literary contribution is much needed for us fast-paced millennial parents who are working hard to raise the next generation!

—**Kaila Maguire**, certified childbirth educator, babywearing educator, gift registry expert, and podcaster, co-author with Jess Myhre of *Ruby June Has a Diner in Her Room!*

Jason has produced an essential resource that will empower families to be safer and happier. This comprehensive guide to all aspects of family safety is not only written in helpful and accessible language ... it provides insights and information to allow you to make the best decisions for your own family and situation. It is not a directive and judgmental handbook—it is a friendly and supportive guide you will enjoy reading and from which you will gain a ton of tips to avoid everything from pitfalls to predators. You can read it cover to cover, you can dip in and out to focus on your current concerns–whether that be security when travelling, mental health, bullying, or living in a positive state of awareness instead of fear and paranoia.

As someone who has worked in education for thirty years, I can heartily recommend this brilliant book that should be on every family's wish list. It is definitely one you'll want to order for yourself but also makes a perfect present to protect those you love.

—**Mary Stevens**, MA (Oxon) PGCE, 4th dan British Combat Karate Association, author of *Warrior Monkeys*, co-author of *Animal Instincts Children's Self Protection Programme*, project manager for Fairfight.nl India (self-defense for vulnerable young women), 500Rising UK, and Europe Women's Self-Defence Advisory Group

In a world where you can get advice on anything from just about anyone, many people struggle to identify true experts. Don't get caught up Googling your questions on how to keep your family safe. Take it straight from the masters of their craft. This book will put you in a position to take the tangible, practical steps needed to ensure your family's well-being. This is one of those books that you NEED if you are a parent. There is no more important discipline that you should hone your expertise in than parenting, so take the first step and grab this important book!

—**Alexander Bromley**, Verbal Judo Institute, homicide detective, SWAT teamcrisis negotiator

Unfortunately, we live in a world filled with hidden dangers. Luckily, an ounce of prevention is worth a pound of cure. That is why those who wish to protect themselves and the ones they love would do well to read *Safest Family on the Block*. In this book, Jason Brick addresses many important aspects of everyday life that most people put very little thought into, but should! *Safest Family on the Block* examines potential safety concerns and simple solutions for nearly all aspects of modern life. The impressive range of subjects covered is very diverse and complex, but each is addressed in a condensed format that is well presented and easy to read. Brick's occasional use of humor helps to blunt the seriousness of the topics, and the wide variety of issues he addresses ensures that there is something important in this book for everyone.

> —**Joe Varady**, 7th degree black belt, author of *The Art and Science of Self-Defense*, *The Art and Science of Stick Fighting*, *The Art and Science of Staff Fighting*, and *The Art and Science of Sword Fighting*

I have studied and taught self-defense for my entire adult life, and as a result, I have come to understand that real self-defense is found in prevention. Avoiding a potentially dangerous situation before it ever has the chance to become dangerous is self-defense at the highest level. For this reason, I give my wholehearted endorsement to the work of Jason Brick and *Safest Family on the Block*. Each tip is a reminder for all of us to be alert, aware, and to be as present as we are able, as ANYTHING safety-focused we do before any sort of event is one-thousand times more valuable than anything we can do afterward. Knowledge and prevention are the ultimate tools of personal and family protection. Be proactive.

> —**Tom Callos**, founder of Ultimate Black Belt Test

Safest Family on the Block is smart and contains practical information that everyone (anyone) can use. Smart is not a word I use lightly, because for me, something earns the label of smart only when it hits that rare intersection of intellectually stimulating, actually useful, and readily applicable. You will benefit from the content as well as the way the information is presented.

> —**Katherine A. Wieczerza**, 9th dan black belt, director of Goju-Shorei Weapons System, contributor to the book, *There I Was...When Nothing Happened: True Tales of Real Self-Defense from Professionals in the Field*

Safest Family on the Block

Safest Family on the Block

101 Tips, Tricks, Hacks, and Habits to Protect Your Family

Jason Brick

YMAA Publication Center
Wolfeboro, NH USA

YMAA Publication Center, Inc.
PO Box 480
Wolfeboro, New Hampshire 03894
1-800-669-8892 • info@ymaa.com • www.ymaa.com
ISBN: 9781594399909 (print) • ISBN: 9781594399916 (ebook) • ISBN: 9781594399923 (hardcover)

Edited by Doran Hunter
Cover design by Axie Breen
This book is typeset in Adobe Garamond and Open Sans.

20250320

Publisher's Cataloging in Publication

Names: Brick, Jason, 1972- author.

Title: Safest family on the block : 101 tips, tricks, hacks, and habits to protect your family / by Jason Brick.

Description: Wolfeboro, NH USA : YMAA Publication Center, [2025]

Identifiers: ISBN: 9781594399909 (softcover) | 9781594399923 (hardcover) | 9781594399916 (ebook) | LCCN: 2024952421

Subjects: LCSH: Safety education. | Families--Safety measures. | Accidents--Prevention. | Fire prevention. | Home accidents--Prevention. | Crime prevention. | Travel--Safety measures. | Emergency management. | Self-protective behavior. | BISAC: FAMILY & RELATIONSHIPS / Parenting / General. | FAMILY & RELATIONSHIPS / Life Stages / School Age. | HOUSE & HOME / Safety & Security. | SELF-HELP / Safety & Security / General.

Classification: LCC: HV676.A2 B75 2025 | DDC: 363.1--dc23

TABLE OF CONTENTS

FOREWORD

If you were born in the 80s and 90s, the safety lessons we learned do not necessarily apply to our kids. The age-old advice that kept kids playing in the neighborhood until the streetlights came on doesn't work in 2025.

In other words, what we were taught as kids needs to be modernized.

We as parents are learning as we go what it's like to protect our children in person and online. That's why we need to have a well-rounded mindset when it comes to protecting our kids.

I've always been happy to have numerous podcast conversations with Jason. Whether I'm on his *Safest Family on the Block* or he's on my podcast for *The Secure Dad,* we always seem to compliment and expand each other's knowledge.

In one such conversation, Jason referred to situational awareness as being "tactically curious." This is a phrase that has stuck with me for years. It's a great way to think about the world around you how it affects your family's safety. This book will help you to be tactically curious about what's happening in world around your family.

As parents, we constantly juggle the responsibility of keeping our families safe in an ever-changing world. That's why Jason Brick's *Safest Family on the Block: 101 Tips, Tricks, Hacks, and Habits to Protect Your Family* is more than just a book—it's a lifeline for families seeking peace of mind in a seemingly chaotic world.

Jason brings a truly unique perspective to the important subject of family safety. A seasoned world traveler, martial arts instructor, and devoted father, his experiences provide him with an unparalleled ability to see danger—and opportunity—from every angle.

Each chapter of this book distills his wealth of knowledge into practical, easy-to-follow advice that empowers parents to act confidently and decisively. His insight stems not only from his professional background but also from the lessons learned in his personal journey, balancing family life and the ever-present role of protector.

One of the critical lessons of this book is how it challenges outdated concepts, especially in the relationship between children and strangers. For generations, parents relied on simple, catch-all advice like "don't talk to strangers" and "stranger danger" to keep kids safe. While well-intentioned, this approach no longer fits the complex, interconnected reality our children face today.

Jason adeptly redefines the stranger-danger narrative, replacing it with a more nuanced, empowering approach. He encourages parents to teach their kids not just fear but discernment and to gain their own experience.

Instead of blanket warnings, Jason focuses on helping children understand how to assess real situations, read social cues, and trust their intuition. He invites parents to rethink outdated advice, helping them prepare their children to navigate the world with awareness and confidence rather than anxiety.

Jason's guidance is also refreshingly realistic. He doesn't sell or profit from fear or overwhelm. Instead, he offers thoughtful steps that make a great impact over time. This book is about showing parents that they don't have to be perfect or know everything—they just need the right tools and strategies to get started.

As a father, Jason's perspective is both relatable and empathetic. He understands the challenges modern parents face, from addressing online safety to dealing with walking the route at school while still allowing kids the freedom to explore and grow. His approach is never heavy-handed; instead, it's rooted in collaboration and communication. Jason encourages parents to work with their kids and to lead by example.

One of the most impactful takeaways from this book, and our podcast discussions, is the reminder that safety is a family effort. It's not just about the actions parents take, but also about the habits, values, and skills they pass on to their children.

Jason invites families to view safety as a partnership, where everyone has a role to play. This perspective not only strengthens family bonds but also ensures that everyone is better equipped to handle what life throws at them.

By the time you finish this book, you'll find yourself thinking differently about what it means to protect your family, which is a good thing. You'll realize that safety isn't about building walls or avoiding the world—it's about engaging with it more thoughtfully.

The journey to becoming the safest family on the block begins with small, intentional steps. Whether you're implementing one of Jason's home security tips, teaching your kids about situational awareness, or revisiting outdated advice, each action brings you closer to the peace of mind every parent craves. With this book in hand, you have everything you need to create a safer, more resilient family.

So, as you turn the page and begin this journey, know that you're not just learning from an expert—you're learning from someone who's been in your shoes. Jason Brick understands what it means to love, protect, and guide a family. His insights are your invitation to step into the role of protector with clarity and courage. I wish you the best of luck.

—Andy Murphy
Founder, The Secure Dad

A family safety advocate with years of experience helping families live safer lives, Andy Murphy shows parents how to protect their family at home, in public, and online. Find out more at TheSecureDad.com.

INTRODUCTION

When I first heard that Jason Brick was working on a new book, I knew it would be something special. Jason is one of those rare individuals who can distill the chaos and challenges of life into actionable insights that genuinely make a difference. His background, his expertise, and—most importantly—his commitment to helping others improve their lives set him apart as a leader and a mentor. It's my absolute honor to introduce his latest work to you.

Jason and I share a common mission: empowering parents to become the best version of themselves. As parents, we understand the weight of responsibility we carry, and the profound impact we have on the people around us. What makes Jason's voice so compelling is that he doesn't just talk about personal growth as a concept. He lives it. He breathes it. And, through this book, he shares his process with you in a way that is both accessible and transformative.

Why This Book Matters. We're living in an era of unprecedented demands on those of us who have families. Expectations are higher than ever, and the tools for navigating life's complexities often feel like they're lagging behind. Between balancing careers, supporting our families, and carving out time for our own well-being, it's easy to feel stretched thin—sometimes to the point of breaking.

This is where Jason's work shines. This book doesn't offer surface-level advice or generic platitudes. Instead, it's a guide for digging deep, reassessing priorities, and creating meaningful change in your life. Whether you're looking to strengthen your relationships, enhance your career, or simply find clarity amidst the noise, you'll find actionable steps here that can make a real difference.

One of the aspects I admire most about Jason's approach is his ability to bridge the gap between theory and practice. He understands that reading about change is easy; implementing it is hard. That's why every chapter of this book is crafted with intention. Jason doesn't just tell you what to do—he equips you with the tools, strategies, and mindset shifts you need to make it happen.

Jason's Unique Perspective. Jason's diverse background is one of the key factors that make this book stand out. He's a lifelong martial artist, a dedicated coach, and a prolific writer. Each of these roles has shaped his understanding of personal growth and resilience in profound ways.

As a martial artist, Jason has spent decades honing the discipline and focus required to succeed in one of the world's most demanding practices. He's learned how to navigate failure, push through discomfort, and emerge stronger on the other side—all lessons he brings into this book.

As a coach, Jason has guided countless individuals through their own transformative journeys. He knows what works and, just as importantly, what doesn't. His insights are grounded in real-world experience, which means you're not just reading theory; you're learning from someone who has walked the path and helped others do the same.

As a writer, Jason has a gift for clarity. He knows how to communicate complex ideas in a way that resonates and inspires action. This book is no exception. From the very first page, you'll feel like Jason is speaking directly to you, offering guidance that is both practical and deeply personal.

The Core Themes. At its heart, this book is about transformation. But it's not about a one-size-fits-all approach. Jason recognizes that each person's journey is unique, and he offers a framework that you can adapt to your own circumstances.

The book is divided into clear, actionable sections that address the key areas of life where men often struggle:

1. **Mindset**—Jason dives into the mental blocks that hold so many of us back and offers strategies for overcoming them. You'll learn how to shift your perspective, break free from limiting beliefs, and cultivate a mindset of growth and resilience.

2. **Relationships**—Whether it's your marriage, your role as a father, or your friendships, Jason provides insights for building deeper, more meaningful connections. He understands the challenges parents face in expressing vulnerability and shows you how to embrace it as a strength.

3. **Purpose and Passion**—So many of us feel stuck in a rut, unsure of their direction or disconnected from their passions. Jason helps you rediscover what drives you and align your life with your core values.

4. **Physical and Emotional Health**—True transformation starts from within. Jason addresses the importance of self-care—not as a luxury, but as a necessity. From fitness to mental well-being, he gives you the tools to build a strong foundation for every other aspect of your life.

5. **Legacy**—Finally, Jason challenges you to think about the mark you want to leave on the world. This isn't just about your career or your achievements; it's about the impact you have on the people who matter most.

My Personal Takeaway. As someone who has spent years building a community of men striving for greatness, I've seen firsthand how powerful the right guidance can be. What Jason has created with this book is more than just a roadmap—it's a lifeline for anyone who feels stuck, overwhelmed, or uncertain about their next steps.

Reading this book reminded me of why I started *The Dad Edge* in the first place. It's easy to get caught up in the grind of daily life and lose sight of what really matters. Jason's words are a wake-up call, a reminder that we have the power to shape our lives and create the future we want.

But transformation doesn't happen passively. It requires effort, intention, and a willingness to step outside your comfort zone. If you're ready to put in the work, this book will meet you where you are and guide you every step of the way.

A Call to Action. I want to end this introduction with a challenge. As you read Jason's book, don't just absorb the information—act on it. Highlight the sections that resonate with you. Write down your goals. Commit to the changes you want to make, no matter how small they might seem.

Jason has poured his heart and soul into this work, not to impress you, but to empower you. The tools are here. The insights are here. Now it's up to you to take the first step.

Jason, thank you for creating this incredible resource. Your work is going to change lives, and I'm honored to be a part of introducing it to the world.

To everyone reading: buckle up. This isn't just a book—it's a journey. And I can't wait to see where it takes you.

—**Larry Hagner,**
Founder, The Dad Edge

How This Happened

In early spring of 2007, I suddenly became the dad of a seven-year-old boy. This wasn't a "try for a year, then have nine months warning" situation. It was an in-family adoption where the parent was suddenly no longer medically capable of full-time parenting.

I had recently earned a fourth-degree black belt in my highest-ranking martial art. I'd been a bouncer and a bodyguard and had competed in wrestling, full-contact karate, Muay Thai, and Brazilian jujitsu. With my equally athletic and overconfident college roommate, I'd explored some sketchy corners of the world and come back with stories and scars. I'd had guns pointed at me twice and a knife in me once. I thought I was a badass.

But there I was, practicing weapon disarms with some very smart and knowledgeable experts. As I walked through the techniques, I noticed that many of them put the business end of the weapon past me at about hip level. The height of a child's head.

The height of *my* child's head.

That, and a lot of other thinking, made me realize how poorly all my training and experience had prepared me to protect other people. Especially small, mostly helpless people who relied on me for their safety. And that's just the self-defense stuff, which I had already spent more than twenty years practicing.

The other skills I was far worse at. First aid, fire prevention, nutrition, communication, cyber safety, bullying…they were things I sometimes paid lip service to, but they weren't up to the standards my newfound responsibility deserved.

I was lucky enough to have great instructors, teachers, mentors, and role models. One thing they all taught me in different ways was that learning is the best way to overcome challenges.

So I set my mind to learning how to best protect my child. I found experts in everything I could think of about protecting my kids, and then I talked to other experts those experts recommended. I tested their advice and came back with questions, then more questions, then more questions after that.

Thirteen years, another kid, a divorce, a new career in journalism, a new marriage, a year with my kids in Southeast Asia and another with them in Crete, and a bunch of other stuff later, COVID happened.

During the lockdowns, I started my show. In *Safest Family on the Block*, I use the lens of my experience as a martial artist, journalist, and parent to interview the most knowledgeable people I can find on every conceivable topic of family safety. As of this writing, I'm closing in on three years and one hundred episodes.

This book is a distillation of what I learned during those interviews. It's not everything those generous experts had to say, but it's the most valuable for most families.

I hope it does as much for you as learning all of it did for me.

SECTION 1

GOLDEN RULES

Introduction by Joe Borovicka

A military veteran with experience on four continents, Joe Borovicka teaches evidence-based self-protection and fear management to organizations, families, and individuals. Find out more at readinessrx.com.

I'm thrilled to introduce this essential section. I say "essential" because after three decades of martial arts training, I realized that mastering principles was more important than collecting techniques.

Your minimum effective dose of practical self-protection knowledge must include basic principles for success.

For example, during pre-deployment combat training in the US military, my group had a special-forces medic instructing us. I'll call him Max. Once Max realized we'd all had basic combat first-aid training and field experience, he threw away the checklist. He built a training scenario and allowed us to gather all the information ourselves and choose the best way to save the casualty.

In the skillset of self-protection, you don't want "the ultimate move" that dominates any situation. What you want is to truly see the situation and make a decision based on sound principles.

The Golden Rules described here are simple to understand and give direction to your personal safety regardless of where you are and what you're doing.

1 Be Alert for Change

By the time I wrote this book, I'd interviewed over one hundred experts in safety disciplines ranging from crime prevention, to firefighting, to suicide counselling, to communication, to bullying, to emergency response.

These were all leaders in varying fields, with different passions, perspectives, and training. Despite this, they agreed on a few key points. The most common and most important was this:

Change is the first sign of danger.

You hear a lot of safety and security people talking about situational awareness and how important it is. The people saying that are right, but only half right. Awareness is important, but only works when we know *what to be aware about.*

Think about a quiet bar, maybe late on a weeknight in a business hotel. The quiet doesn't mean it's dangerous. Now think about a college bar on a Friday night with a rock band playing. The noise doesn't mean it's dangerous. Your awareness of the noise level doesn't give you valuable safety information.

But what if that quiet hotel bar suddenly became noisy? Or if the crowd at the college bar all hushed at once? In either case, that change in the noise level tells you it's time to pay closer attention.

Your warning wasn't the level of noise. It was how the level of noise changed one moment to the next. The same would be true if it was different from what you expected; for example, walking into a shop that's usually crowded but finding it empty.

This doesn't just apply to avoiding a bar fight. Those experts I listed, and others, all had some version of this advice.

- The suicide counsellor said to look for changes in how often or from what your child feels joy.
- The bullying expert said to watch for changes in behavior, grades, or before-school routine.
- The firefighter advised learning the fire safety protocols in new places when we change where we spend time.
- The communications coach said to be aware of when and how the tone of discussions shifts, both the conversation itself and your attitude within it.
- An internet safety specialist said to pay attention when your child's online behavior changes, including body language while using a connected device.
- A parenting coach suggested remaining alert to when our state of mind changes so we know the best times to do the heavy lifting in our relationship with our kids.

I could go on. Of the hundred episodes of my show, maybe a dozen didn't touch on change as an important early warning signal of danger to our families.

Don't Fear Change. This advice is good news for people who want to be alert about danger because it means you can relax your vigilance from time to time. That "head on a swivel" approach many self-defense experts recommend comes from police and military training. It's important for them, potentially lifesaving.

But they apply it in the context of a dangerous job, where they get to stop work and be safe after a while. Their hyper-alert status is temporary. It has to be, because it's exhausting.

You don't get much time off as a parent. Staying that kind of alert isn't sustainable or healthy. By staying alert for change, you can relax a bit when nothing's out of place and save your energy for when it matters.

Finding Baseline. The tactical crowd uses the term "baseline" to describe the normal expectation for a situation, like the noise level you expect in that bar, or your child's usual grades in different subjects, or how much of the computer screen they let you see while they're online.

I disagree with them about keeping your head on a swivel every second whenever you're out in the world. I do agree that understanding the baseline for the people you love and the places you go is important for staying safe.

Take some time to think about, talk with your co-parents about, maybe write down the baselines you observe about your loved ones, home, work, and the places you often go. By simply expressing what's normal, you reinforce how alert you will be for changes from that baseline...and that extra alertness where it matters will make you all safer.

2 Worry Less About Crime

When many of us think about family safety, our minds go to crime, but let's look at the leading causes of death according to the CDC.

- Among adults of parenting age: unintentional injury, cancer, heart disease, suicide, and liver disease.
- Among young children: unintentional injury, congenital diseases, homicide, suicide, and cancer.
- Among tweens, teens, and young adults: unintentional injury, suicide, homicide, cancer, and heart disease.
- Among seniors: cancer, heart disease, unintentional injury, stroke, and chronic lower respiratory disease.

The leading causes of injury across all age groups are various types of unintentional injury, split up into labels like "Unintentional Fall," "Unintentional Motor Vehicle—Occupant," "Unintentional Cut/ Pierce," and "Unintentional Other Specified." Assault doesn't even show up for young children or seniors and tops out at number-eight among adults and older teens.

Based on all of this, focusing on crime prevention is a bad allocation of resources when it comes to keeping our families safe.

It's Even Better Than That. Homicide shows up as a leading cause of death among young children, teens, tweens, and young adults. That's scary, and unmitigatedly awful when it happens.

But diving deeper into the numbers reveals a reassuring fact. Those homicide rates also aren't high. They just turn up in the top five because people of that age group very rarely die from anything.

Death and injury from crime is rare across all age groups, even the ones where it shows up among the top causes.

Great. Now I'm Even *More* Worried. My point here isn't to get everybody worried about crime *plus* illness, accidents, cancer, and genetic disorders. There's a lot of pain and not much comfort down that road.

My point here is to focus our efforts on the things that matter most—to focus less on crimes that rarely happen and more on car accidents, kitchen safety, and lifestyle practices that will keep our family happier, healthier, and safer for longer.

This book contains several tips about avoiding, resisting, and surviving crime. Those tips only represent about 10 percent of the book. The rest are about addressing all the other hazards and risks that threaten our kids, partners, elders, and other loved ones. Hopefully, you'll come out of it with a similar scale of prioritization for your own safety efforts.

It's Not as Much Fun. I think our focus on crime prevention comes from two places. First, the press and our entertainment suggest crime is everywhere.

News stories about mass shootings, gang violence, and random assaults sell better than reporting on traffic accidents, fire deaths, and backyard barbecue injuries. Nobody's making summer blockbusters about a suburban family who eats right and gets plenty of exercise.

Second, violent crime isn't fun to think about, but it can be fun to prepare for. Martial arts classes are *fun*. Range time is *fun*. There's a feeling of empowered accomplishment to installing security cameras and setting up an escape plan.

Compare and contrast that to stocking up enough water for a week without power, putting on your seatbelt, or getting serious about your social media information security. That stuff is more important, because it protects you more often—but I'll be the first to admit it's less fun.

But we're parents. Doing the less fun thing for a better result is part of what we signed on for.

3   Live by Example

Here's a frustrating fact about parenting. Our kids don't listen much, but they are *always* watching. It's frustrating because that's how they catch us when we don't walk our talk.

I grew up in the 1980s, during which time there was a famous public service commercial on television about not using drugs. It featured a heated exchange between father and son. When the father asked, "Where did you learn to do this?" about the son's drug use, the son replied, "I learned it from watching you!"

The ad's a bit over the top, but that message applies to so much more than drugs. How your child wears a seatbelt, they learn by watching what you do with your seatbelt. How your child thinks and talks about school, they learn from watching how you talk about your education and theirs. How they treat their romantic partners, how often they tell the truth, whether or not they text while driving. Whether they wear a helmet while riding a bike.

All of it, they learn by watching you.

Which means it's our job as parents to live by example, demonstrating the safety habits and practicing the techniques we think are important. First they see us do it, then they imitate us. Eventually they'll remind us to do it...and as adults, they'll teach the same things to our grandchildren.

The Next Level. When I work with clients or present at events, the biggest questions I get asked have to do with how to talk to kids about safety without scaring them.

I understand the worry. Many parents fear that discussing potential dangers will plant the idea of those dangers in a little one's mind. I'll go into that in more detail later, but for now...

When our kids see us looking both ways when crossing the street, at first they don't think about it at all. Later on they might ask about it. When we tell them we do that so we're safer from being hit by a car, one of two things happens. In one case, they've already been exposed to the idea of that danger, and you give them a new tool to help prevent it. In the other, this is the first time they've thought about the risk of being hit by a car, and their first exposure to this potentially scary idea comes with the knowledge that you are already doing something about it and teaching them a way to be safer, too.

That seems to me less scary and more empowering than any other way to discuss safety with our kids.

4 Stranger Doesn't Equal Danger

You grew up hearing this mantra everywhere: from your parents, your teachers, your pastor, on the news…everywhere.

Don't Talk to Strangers.

Strangers are dangerous. They lurk in vans distributing candy. Do not trust them under any circumstances. They offer treats or ask for help and take us away from our families forever. Stranger equals danger.

It's not true.

No matter how well-intended the adults who told us this were, they were wrong. This was probably the worst advice we got as kids, and we shouldn't pass it on to our children.

Why?

I'm glad you asked.

We Do Not Model This. Adults talk to strangers all the time: the guy at the checkout stand, our Uber driver, random people at the bus stop. Talking to strangers is a normal part of human interaction. Kids watch more than they listen. When we say one thing but do another, it's predictable which they'll imitate.

It Does Not Work. Research over the past four decades has shown this messaging makes no difference in how likely children are to be victimized. This is largely because most intentional harm to children comes from adults they know.

It Presents a Terrifying World. The overwhelming majority of people, which means the overwhelming majority of strangers, are good of heart and won't hurt children. "Don't talk to strangers" describes a world where everybody they don't know is a threat. Our children deserve better than to grow up thinking that's how the world is.

It Steals Their Agency. If a child needs help, they must get it from a stranger. If somebody they know is available, they don't need help. They're getting help.

Children should learn to approach strangers for help and how to get what they need when their adults aren't around. Leaving them afraid to ask strangers for assistance robs them of the tools they need to be safe in emergencies.

Put that all together, and it's clear we shouldn't teach the old lie of stranger danger. But what should we teach instead?

Focus on Safe Strangers. We can teach our children what kind of strangers to ask when they need help.

The simplest advice is to find another parent and ask them for help. This is statistically the safest and most helpful kind of stranger for a child to approach. Parents are rarely predators, and most will stop at very little to reunite a lost child with their people.

It's not always evident which adults are parents, so we can teach the handy guideline: "If you can't find your family, find somebody else's family."

Teach your kids to memorize this and to look for adults with children. That might be actual parents with kids, but it could be grandparents, aunts, uncles, nannies, a day care group, or any number of other family constellations. The point is, if your child goes to an adult with children for help, that is their best bet for safety and assistance.

Practice What You Teach. After we teach this lesson, it's important to practice it. When you're out to eat or waiting in line, ask your kids who in the room they would go to for help. Ask why about whoever they identify.

This conversation prepares our children to act for their own safety. If our children lose track of us in public, they will be under tremendous stress. People of all ages are rarely successful under stress with things they don't practice.

5 Be Curious and Mindful

Let's talk about the Cooper Color Codes, a concept taught in self-defense circles as a way of structuring situational awareness. The colors are:

- **Condition White:** Fully relaxed and mostly unaware, a condition to be in only under safe conditions like when you're locked in your home.
- **Condition Yellow:** A relaxed state of alertness, ideally your default state.
- **Condition Orange:** Awareness of and focusing on a potential threat you have spotted.
- **Condition Red:** Confirmed something is a threat, then taking action to avoid or engage with it.

Pretty cool, huh? It helps people organize their thought process around awareness. It comes from an exalted military personality. It has a tactical, official feel.

I'm not much of a fan.

Wait, What? The Cooper Color Codes are a good way to think about threats and awareness, but a bad way to live our lives.

The system was originally designed by a military man, for use by military and law enforcement. It then got spread to civilians, but it's not intended or appropriate for you and me.

Military and law enforcement go out on shift or patrol in dangerous circumstances where they need their awareness dialed in tight. Those shifts begin and end, and in between their shifts they get to relax. Being this focused on threats and danger is exhausting and rough on mental health.

As parents, we're on shift almost all the time. It's neither reasonable nor healthy to keep up a "head on a swivel, back to the wall" state of alertness for all of the hours we're responsible for our kids.

A Page from a Different Book. Civilian parents living in the developed world shouldn't look to Cooper and his ilk. They're good people doing their best, and they've saved lives. But their context is not our context.

Instead, take a page from Thich Nhat Hanh, famed Buddhist poet, philosopher, and activist. He teaches living mindfully, in the present moment, as much as possible.

Mindfulness means to focus our attention on what is happening now instead of cringing about past mistakes or worrying about the future. It creates a relaxed and joyful state of awareness and engagement with the people, things, and events around us.

As Thich Nhat Hanh says, "In mindfulness, one is not only restful and happy, but alert and awake. Meditation is not evasion; it is a serene encounter with reality."

That serene encounter with reality includes spotting criminal and accidental hazards as they approach your family, just like the Cooper Color Codes. But it's less taxing on our energy and emotions.

As a bonus, it keeps us aware of all the beautiful things. We spot the sketchy guy loitering in the parking lot, but we also catch sunsets, flowers, and that kitten who wants a quick scratch behind the ears.

Even better, it helps us focus on all the little interactions and joys we can have with our kids. And it helps us focus on them, showing our little ones they are the most important things in our lives.

6 Put Down the Phone

There's a lot of panic about how bad screens are for our kids. Too much screen time has been linked to increased anxiety, reduced attention spans, and general moral turpitude. Some of those links are supported by science. Others are the fears of a few social influencers or long-standing parenting boogeymen dressed up for the twenty-first century.

But we're not here to talk about that. We're here to talk about what phones do to *us*. For every real worry about our kids and their phones, there's a corresponding one for parents. Here are the four I've seen doing the most harm.

The Obvious. Let's start with something we all already know. Using our screens while driving is bad, and something most of us should do less.

We already know this, but it's easy to forget in the moment. It's a guilty slip I make so often, I have an agreement where if my oldest son catches me slipping, he picks the music for the rest of the drive.

It's surprisingly effective. If you have trouble with staying off your phone behind the wheel, consider recruiting your kids.

The Bad Guys Are Watching. In a 1981 study, criminologists Betty Grayson and Morris Stein showed a variety of inmates videotapes of people walking and asked them which people they would target.

Regardless of offense, gender, race, or other indicators, they generally chose the same people. When looking at what those people had in common, Grayson and Stein noticed similarities in body language, gait, and attitude. Most of the chosen victims showed a marked lack of visible awareness.

Looking at our phones takes attention from the outside world and tells criminals we're vulnerable. It also puts a high-value, easily portable item to steal right where they can see it.

Alain Burrese, former US Army sniper and current safety expert, puts it like this: "Get your head out of your apps!"

Something Precious. It's important that our kids trust that they can come to us with problems. One way to ensure that is to show that we're listening and give them our undivided attention when they ask for it.

If they're talking to us, especially if it's yet another rambling story about what happened on a YouTube video or in their new favorite video game, it's tempting to check our phones.

I get it, but that sends a clear message about how much of our attention we think their thoughts are worth. It's on us to make our children certain that we value them more than we do our phones.

Social Signals. A lot of time spent on phones is taken up with social media, which can be great. Those small daily connections can strengthen relationships with people you care about who don't share your zip code.

On the other hand, most of us post too much information where anybody can see it. We show what valuables are in our homes, when we'll go on vacation, and where our kids will be this evening. We share birthdays, interests, hobbies, and other clues that help identity thieves and stalkers do what they do best.

I'm not saying we shouldn't use social media while on our phones. I'm only suggesting we ask ourselves if we want the whole world to know what we're about to put out there.

One Way to Look at It. For a lot of us, our phones have become something we do *in addition to whatever else we're doing at the time.* We check social media while chatting. We stream shows while doing laundry. We send email while watching a movie.

I propose that we change that paradigm. When it's time to do stuff on our phones, we do stuff on our phones. When it's time to do other things, we do those other things.

It will take some getting used to, but most of us are old enough to remember a time without smartphones. We'll just be getting back to how we were before these miraculous tools were part of our lives.

7 Focus on Who They'll Become

One common bad habit for parents, myself included, is our tendency to borrow trouble from the future. When our kids do something that isn't a huge deal right now, sometimes we flash forward to what that behavior might mean for them in grade school, as a teen, in college, or as an adult. We see our little ones doing something that's age appropriate, but we think about what it might mean many years from now.

And honestly, we panic. We set up consequences, end up in conflicts, and generally have a rough time over something that's going to fade with time, growth, and maturity.

Take for example drama around what they eat at dinner. Yes, we know that an adult who's a picky eater will hurt their friendships, romantic relationships, and even job opportunities. Yes, we're justified in thinking how unpleasant it will be to have to deal with this every night for the next ten years.

But how much does it really matter? Is it our best move to pick a fight around whether or not they eat that broccoli? Or is it better to intentionally set rules that avoid the drama, and play a longer game about nutrition and table manners?

At best, picking the fight means losing a few minutes or hours that could have been much more pleasant while still not hurting our kids' future prospects. At worst, it erodes the trust and communication between us and our children and makes them more vulnerable to bullies and predators.

This Present Moment. Instead of worrying about who our kids will be, we can take a page from mindfulness. Focus on who we are in that moment. What goals and priorities are we modeling? What are we teaching our kids about how to talk with, and be in conflict with, the people they love? How safe and loved do they feel when they make mistakes, and how do we teach them to overcome challenges? Our little ones are learning machines. It's basically all they do. Let's give them the best us to learn from.

It also helps to remember who they are in that moment. A toddler, teenager, or young adult still lacks a well-developed brain capable of self-regulation and understanding realistic cause and effect. Some of the biggest conflicts we have with our little ones are when we expect something of them that they're just not ready for.

Supportive Communication. Who they'll be versus who you're afraid they'll be is an opportunity to practice the skill of supportive communication with our kids. A great example of this in action is the careers they want to pursue.

We need to meet our kids where they are. We may want something for them that's very different from what they see happening in their lives. We might want that because it gives them opportunities we didn't have, or because it lets them fulfill dreams we never pursued, or for any number of other reasons. Most of those reasons have to do with our happiness, not theirs.

If we can have those conversations with active listening, understanding, and respect for our children's agency, then we show them each time how we'll act when they deliver us other kinds of news we might not like. If you've read this far, you've already seen the importance of keeping those lines of communication open, warm, and loving.

8 Never Go to a Second Location

This piece might be the hardest thing you'll read in this book. It's also among the least likely to come up. That said, it's important and not well reflected in the media or even advice from many "experts."

Crime Scene #2 is what police call the place where a criminal takes a victim after the initial point of contact. In the movies, it's where the tension ratchets up and the good guy ultimately triumphs. In the real world, nothing good happens at Crime Scene #2.

I'll paint the picture with an example. You're in a parking garage late at night, about to get in your car. A criminal steps out from hiding and points a gun at you. He demands your car keys and tells you to get in the car with him, that he'll let you go if you do what he tells you. He says that if you don't, he will shoot you right there.

With a weapon aimed at you, you're scared. You're wondering if you'll ever see your family again. You're tempted to do as he says. What's worse, I've seen journalists recommend on live TV that you should cooperate. But that's the last thing you should do. I said it before, but it's important enough to say again, in big letters.

Nothing Good Happens at Crime Scene #2. If the criminal is actually willing to shoot you in a parking garage, what do you think he has planned for you when he has you alone wherever he wants to take you? He will not keep his promise to let you go.

Likewise, if he does shoot you in that parking garage for refusing, you are much closer to medical help than if he shoots you in whatever secluded, private area he has in mind.

One last point on this. Think, very briefly, about the kind of death a criminal has in mind for you if he wants to take you some place private where he won't be interrupted for hours or even days. Compare that to the worst-case scenario of being shot in a parking lot while he flees the scene.

Nothing good happens at Crime Scene #2.

Never Agree. Never Go. We've established that you should never go with a criminal who wants to transport you to a second location. What can you do instead? They're threatening you with a weapon, and they may intend to use it.

Run away. Say nothing but scream. Do nothing but run. Every foot you put between you and them exponentially increases the chances they will give up the chase. Every decibel you put out in the world makes it more likely they'll cut and run. Accuracy with pistols from just a few feet away is very low even for police officers, so each extra step makes them less able to act on the threat. Run. Scream. Run and scream some more until you're safe.

If you can't run, fight. Attack immediately, without warning, and with everything you have. Scream and hit and kick and bite. Do not stop harming your attacker until they run away or stop moving entirely, or you have a chance to escape.

What About the Kids? Everything I said above is all well and good if you're by yourself, but kids change some of what's realistically possible. They also up the emotional ante, making most parents easier to intimidate.

The best response if a criminal tries to take you and your children to Crime Scene #2 depends on their age and mobility.

Infants and toddlers are portable for most people, so the advice doesn't change. Pick up your child and, with your body between them and the criminal, run as fast as possible while screaming as loud as you can. The same goes for teens. Most can run faster than us.

That leaves those elementary and early middle school years, where your children are too heavy to carry but also not fast enough to run. I'm going to report two pieces of advice on this. The first is what experts, who learned what they know from victim interviews and forensic aftermaths, advise. The second is the closest thing to that advice they've ever been able to get parents on board with.

The best advice is to run away and leave them behind. Get to safety, call help, then come back to save them. This is the best advice because it means help is on its way. If you don't run and an attacker stops you, nobody's coming, and your children are at the mercy of somebody who just injured or killed their parent in front of them. This is hard even to think about, but the top people in this field—folks like Sandford Strong, Gavin DeBecker, and Rory Miller all agree that this is the plan with the best likelihood of survival for everyone.

Look, I warned you this would be tough to read.

That's what you *should* do. But even though the experts I trust are unanimous about this, they're equally agreed that parents aren't willing to abandon their kids. So here's the second-best advice.

Attack immediately and ferociously while your kids run to get help. Do not talk. Do not hesitate. Do not stop until the person who wanted private time to hurt your children stops moving, or until your kids are safe and you have a chance to join them.

Crime is rare, and this kind of crime against families is among the rarest. If it does enter your life, you now know what to do.

9 Don't Be a Therapist

...or a doctor, or a lawyer, or a teacher, or any of a long list of other professional careers. It's not in anybody's best interests.

I'm going to walk that back a little. As parents, it is our job to fix booboos, give basic legal advice, help with homework, soothe them when they're anxious, mend broken hearts, and other parts of the jobs those professionals I mentioned do. We'd be remiss in our duty if we didn't do those things.

But it's also our job to know when we're in over our heads. Most of us can pull out a splinter, ice a goose egg, and treat a cold...but we can't cure pneumonia or set a broken bone. Most of us can teach our kids where to parallel park but can't beat a speeding ticket. Even when you can, because you happen to be a professional in one of those areas, the best advice is to ask a colleague to take care of your kids because your emotional attachment can make you less effective.

I heard this first during my interview with Karen Letofsky, one of Canada's foremost experts on suicide prevention. Although this advice applies to many safety situations, I think it's most important with mental health.

It's a little like freelance writing, which I did for a living between my time as a martial arts teacher and beginning the *Safest Family on the Block* project. A lot of people underestimate how valuable a professional writer can be on a project. After all, most people write every day. How much better can the professional really be? That makes sense on the surface, but I fed my family for a decade with how much better the professional really is.

Culturally, I think we do that with mental health. We already serve as counselors and advisors. We talk, and listen, and commiserate, and offer tools every day. We know our kids' moods, triggers, joys, and fears. We help with their mental health *all the time*, and mostly with some success. How much better can the professional be?

Add to that the problematic relationship our culture has with getting mental health help. Although the public narrative is getting better, a lot of people still attach an unconscious (or conscious) stigma to it. Some of us still feel like a child who needs therapy is a child whose parents have failed them.

To further muddy these waters, the insurance situation for mental health care can be tricky and confusing. So can getting care even when you're covered or in a financial position to pay for it out of pocket.

Taken altogether, there are a lot of reasons pushing many of us away from getting professional mental health care for our kids. Given that I heard about this first from a suicide counselor, who has seen too many times what happens when this goes wrong, it's my strongly held opinion that we should overcome that instinct. Not every kid who's had a rough time needs counseling. Not every teen who is anxious about the future or depressed about a breakup needs medication. But there comes a time for some families when our well-intentioned, informed help isn't enough.

When that time comes, we all need to be brave enough to see it for what it is, and loving enough to do what we know must be done.

I try to look at it this way. I'm pretty handy. I can repair most things in my house and did a full bedroom remodel from scratch on my own. But I don't understand plumbing, and I'm out of my depth on wiring anything deeper than outlets and light fixtures. When I need something repaired or built that's beyond what I know, I call a professional to do the work. It doesn't mean I'm not handy. It doesn't make me a bad homeowner. It just shows that I'm aware of my skill set and secure enough to call in people with more skills in their area of expertise.

10   Have a Bias Toward Action

Back in 2024, Patrick Van Horne and Jason A. Riley wrote a book called *Left of Bang*. It was an attempt to explain parts of the US Marine Corps Combat Hunter program for use by civilians. Although it had a lot of good information, as a tool for the regular world it was hit-or-miss. It suffered from what I call a "context gap," where the career military authors with combat experience made several inaccurate assumptions about the lives, risks, capabilities, priorities, and mindset of people living civilian life. Still, it had a few excellent insights. The most important of these was to have a bias toward action.

Having a bias toward action means that, under stress or threat, you should make a decision and act on it immediately.

Even if you have incomplete information. Even if you're worried you'll do it wrong. Even if you have an authority figure telling you otherwise. Even if…even if…even if…

You have the right to keep yourself and your family safe. That begins with taking action.

Another Out-of-Context Example. A strong example, but also coming out of military training, is the idea of *getting off the X*. It works like this.

Imagine a diagram of an ambush. The ambushers have their positions marked on the map, behind buildings, bushes, and other places of concealment. On their map they've drawn a big red X. When the target reaches the X, that's when they all attack.

Now, imagine you're a target when the ambush gets sprung. You don't know who's attacking you. You don't know why. You don't know how many there are, what they're armed with, or where they're hiding. You don't know much, and the situation is now literally life-or-death.

The only thing you know for certain is that most ambushes happen when the attacker is in the best possible position and the target is in the worst possible position. That means the absolute worst thing to do is to remain on the X gathering more information.

So you *get off the X*. It doesn't matter which direction you move, or in what way. It doesn't matter who's attacking you, how many there are, or all the rest. The X is the worst possible place you can be, so moving in any direction away from it reliably improves your position. You do that, then figure the rest out.

That's bias toward action.

Putting It Back in Context. For civilian life, the obvious parallel is if you are attacked in an alley. Violent criminals are cowards. They make their attacks when their victim is in the worst possible position. As soon as you realize you are being attacked, move. Move quickly, decisively, with force. Because the criminal attacked you when you were most vulnerable, anywhere you end up next is better than where you were when the attack started.

Like I said, that's the most obvious application of having a bias for action. It goes well beyond that, though:

- If you're uncomfortable with somebody in your child's life, it's better to investigate than to ignore your intuition.
- It's better to create plans for emergencies than to wait until something happens.
- When driving, a proactive stance toward other drivers is better than just managing your vehicle.

- It's better to have an uncomfortable conversation than to avoid it.
- Making that doctor's appointment beats hoping the symptom will go away.

You get the idea. There are few times, and zero emergencies, where taking action is worse than remaining still. Even if your action isn't optimal, it will still be better than doing nothing.

The caveat is that sometimes, as parents, our best action is to stand by while our children make and learn from their own mistakes.

Golden Rules Action Plan

General advice doesn't do much good, especially for people with free time as limited as active parents. Here's a quick checklist of the most vital action items you can start with today about the Golden Rules of family safety.

Do these this week and you're on your way to a safer family:

❏ Choose places in your home to set your phone when you shouldn't be using it.

❏ Find our if your kids' school still teaches "stranger danger," or if they've moved on to better advice.

❏ Commit to taking a long-term point of view when it comes to your kids.

Find an hour soon and take action to become even safer:

❏ Have a conversation with your kids about the kinds of stranger to approach if they need help.

❏ Watch a first aid/CPR/AED training on YouTube with an eye for what you've forgotten, or what's changed since you last learned this skill.

❏ List, for each family member, the safety factors you worry about most when you think about them…

Make time for these important long-term projects to become the safest family on your block:

❏ Create an action plan for each of the factors you listed for each family member.

❏ Talk with your partner about the "baseline" state of the places you go most often.

❏ Read *Peace Is Every Step* by Thich Nhat Hanh to learn about joyful mindfulness. Don't worry. It's a quick read.

FIRE AND ACCIDENT PREVENTION

Introduction by Justin Schorr

Justin Schorr is a rescue captain with the San Francisco Fire Department and is a second-generation, twenty-seven-year veteran of the fire service.

A piercing alarm wakes you from a sound sleep. It isn't the burglar alarm or the neighbor's annoying car alarm, it's a rhythmic three beeps and it isn't letting up. As you begin to sit up, a nasty burning sensation enters your nostrils. You hear cries from your children in the next room. Your house is on fire.

What do you do?

What can you do?

How can you teach your children to do it?

Without a plan, your family may not be able to fully recover from what has already happened. Half awake, struggling to crawl down a hallway is no place to realize that proper planning was a good idea.

While no book, program, or training seminar can completely remove the threat of fire and accidents in the home, a well-prepared and educated family can mitigate and manage many risks.

In this chapter, Jason takes you through many of the most common supplies, techniques, and plans each family should learn and practice.

While the list may not be complete, it directly addresses the top three causes of fires and accidents in the home: men, women, and children.

With his guidance, and that of the experts he consults, your family will know what to do when that alarm sounds in the early morning hours, if you're unable to prevent it in the first place.

11 Practice with Fire Extinguishers

How would you like to exponentially improve your family's fire safety for twenty dollars and half an hour?

That was a rhetorical question. Of course you would. Here's how to do it with a method I use at my house. As far as I've been able to tell, this is a Jason Brick Original, but it's possible I heard it long ago and forgot.

This method solves a serious problem of fire safety. Most safe homes have fire extinguishers. But most homes with fire extinguishers contain exactly zero people who have used one in the past few years.

Fire extinguishers are built for ease of use, but when you're trying to put out a fire is not the time to be looking up instructions on YouTube. If we want those fire extinguishers to do us any good, we need to train and practice with them. Here's how we do that in my home.

Once each year, I buy a new fire extinguisher. We have three in the house. None of them are fancy. They're just the $20 models you can get at Home Depot. We replace the oldest extinguisher in the house with the new one.

The old one we take into the backyard. On the patio, we build a small campfire. We put on gloves and goggles, and everybody in the house takes turns putting out the fire.

Even when my children were very young, they did it with the help of an adult. Now that the youngest is a teenager, everybody in the house is rated for basic fire extinguisher use.

As a bonus, we also get to practice basic fire building, which can be lifesaving in a wilderness situation and is just convenient during family camping trips.

It takes about thirty minutes from start to finish. It teaches important safety skills to my family. It's fun, especially for the young ones, but also for adults. Because something's on fire, there's even a little pressure testing and adrenaline, especially for the younger kids doing it the first few times.

I encourage you to steal this and put it to work for your family. We do it just before July 4th because of fireworks and camping, but any time is a good time.

A Quick Review. If you've never been formally trained on how to use a home fire extinguisher, here are the basics.

For fires smaller than a beach ball, grab your extinguisher. Stand six to eight feet away (between two and four paces). Remember the acronym PASS:

- **Pull** the pin out of the extinguisher, just like the guy did with a grenade in the last war movie you watched.
- **Aim** the extinguisher at the base of the fire. Flames feed from fuel, so you're going to douse the fuel.
- **Squeeze** the trigger to get the extinguisher going.
- **Sweep** the flow across the base of the fire to put out all fuel.

If the extinguisher runs out before the fire is gone, or if the fire grows larger than a beach ball, evacuate and call the fire department.

If you successfully put out the fire, evacuate and call the fire department. The air inside will be full of toxic fumes, and the professionals will check for hot spots to make sure everything is extinguished.

I'd also encourage you to watch one of the dozens of great You-Tube videos on fire extinguisher use before you do your first training. Reading is good, but seeing is better.

12 Manage Your Medications

Most of us are smart and careful about the obvious poisons in our homes. We keep cleaning supplies, rat poison, and motor oil away from small fingers. We talk to our kids about the dangers they pose.

That's good, but it's not where our focus should be.

According to information compiled by the American Poison Control Centers, over-the-counter and prescription medications are the top cause for both child and adult accidental poisonings. They're in childproof bottles, and we keep them up high to prevent this, but those aren't foolproof measures, and many of them look a little too much like candy.

More important, we adults keep putting them in our mouths. Our little ones love to emulate us, to the tune of 60,000 emergency room visits in the US per year for kids who put a beloved grown-up's medicine in their bodies.

This doesn't happen because we're irresponsible. Most parents are aware of the risks associated with kids and medicine and take steps to avoid them. It happens because of a handful of little mistakes shared by parents worldwide who are doing their best.

- We get interrupted in the middle of taking our meds, often by the little ones we want to protect. We go off to handle the crisis of the moment and forget to put them away.
- If we have to dose multiple times a day, we leave our meds within convenient reach. Or we keep a bottle by the bed when we're sick or injured.

- We put our medications up high on a shelf where our cruising toddlers can't reach. It works great, but then we forget to notice that they have grown or become better climbers, or both.
- Sometimes we use a medication, and because we're sick or distracted, we don't make sure the lid is tightly fastened.
- We keep our medication bottles firmly closed and securely stored...but forget that the convenient pill-a-day organizer we put the drugs in every week does not have a childproof lid.
- Visitors in our house, often our parents and our kids' grandparents, have their own medications but no locked cabinet to store them. Those pills are in their carry-on luggage, which kids can access without a problem.
- We get home from the pharmacy or collect our mailed-in refills and leave them on the counter with other artifacts of our errands.
- Over-the-counter medications can be just as dangerous as prescription drugs, but sometimes we forget that and exercise less caution.
- We rely on the physical protections of childproof packaging and secure storage and don't get around to teaching our kids why medicine can be dangerous.

The Good News. All those things I just mentioned can be arranged into a pretty comprehensive *not-to-do list*. If we follow it mindfully and intentionally, we can reduce our kids' chances of accidental drug-related poisonings to next to zero.

As our kids get older, talking to them about what the medications are and what risks are involved helps keep them out of our children's' mouths. Until they reach the "age of reason," though, it's best to physically restrict and control their access as much as we can.

13 Feed Your Local First Responder

Police, firefighters, and EMTs spend their working lives helping and protecting people, including families. More importantly, at least from my perspective, they see on a daily basis what happens when things go wrong. They know where safety systems fail, where parents miss opportunities to protect their children, and what hazards become tragedies most often in their area.

That's something they all have in common, and one of the reasons anxiety, depression, and suicide are so prevalent in all three careers. Their average workday means moving from the worst day of somebody's life to the worst day of somebody else's life, then on to somebody else's worst day.

Another thing they all have in common is they love to eat. And they love to share some of the expertise they've won through years of seeing terrible things so we don't have to.

If you know a first responder, even casually, ask them over for dinner or a weekend lunch. Have some food, share some drinks, and ask them what they wish you knew. This can be informal and casual as part of a larger conversation, a formal training session in one safety skill or another, or anything in between. You'll know best what's appropriate and comfortable for the person you have in mind.

That works for most people but is out of the question for others. If you don't know any first responders, or are so introverted this feels impossible, go to YouTube. Dozens of local fire departments, police forces, and ambulance companies have posted videos where they share what they know.

It's not as good as a personalized conversation with two-way communication, but it's better than nothing.

14 Know Where Your Hot Water Is

Chances are you've heard at least one heart-wrenching story about a baby or toddler going to the hospital to treat second-degree burns they got in a too-hot bathtub. Those stories are real and tragic, as anybody who's spent any time in a burn unit can tell you in graphic detail.

That said, we have two good reasons not to spend too much of our energy worrying about them.

First, we can prevent them entirely by just turning our water heaters down to 100 degrees. That by itself keeps temperatures below serious burn risk, automatically, every time. Parents around the world know how important automatic reflexes are during those sleep-deprived, overwhelmed first few years. It's really that simple.

Second, we need to be with babies and toddlers every second they're in the tub to prevent drowning. If we're in the room and paying attention, we will see signs the water's too hot well before it becomes an issue. We just test the water before putting them in and watch for signs of discomfort throughout.

So, put those together and we don't need to worry much about bathtub water burns. The risk is real, but we've got it covered. What kinds of burns do we need to worry about, then?

Discomfort from Comfort Foods. On my show, I interviewed an old friend who has been a paramedic long enough to run medical response for a major US international airport. He told me that bathtub burns are very rare, but hot water burns showed up in his life about once a week. If those burns aren't happening in the bathtub, what are they from?

They're from our tea and coffee.

Those hot morning beverages are warm and steamy. They look delicious. Mommy and Daddy clearly love the stuff, and we don't often think about them in terms of being a potential hazard. That cuppa is comfort and fuel for us, but if little hands reach up, they can spill so easily.

When that happens, if we're lucky, they burn their hands. If not, the hot liquid pours right onto their face. A combination of turbulence and tea has led my friend to treating second-degree facial burns more than he likes to think about.

It's scary news, but again has a simple solution. Get into the habit of setting down that hot beverage just out of reach. If we're at the table, putting it down in the middle is all it takes. If we're up and about, eye level will do the trick. Manage our to-go cups the same way (those lids will not stand up to an inquisitive child), and we're back on safe, solid ground.

The Stovetop, Too. Coffee and tea aren't the only sources of cooking-related water burns. When we're getting our chef on, we should always keep the pot handles turned toward the back of the stove and out of reach. That way a little one can't pour a vessel of boiling water or hot grease all over themselves while being curious or trying to be helpful.

While we're at it, it's good to always check cooked pasta for little pockets of near-boiling water. Macaroni and shell pastas are particularly nasty culprits here. Both are favorites for our little ones, and both have hollows that can easily catch and keep a burning surprise.

15 Celebrate Family Safety Day

As I write this book, I'm conspiring with several safety experts, martial arts instructors, parenting coaches, nonprofits, and insurance companies to create a brand-new holiday.

The way I see it, we've made holidays for all kinds of things. We have several to celebrate things that happened decades and centuries ago. We have one where we get together to overeat and argue with our relatives. We even have one to celebrate trees. Although it's not an official holiday, a lot of Americans treat Super Bowl Sunday like a national holiday.

If we can celebrate everything from alders to touchdowns with a holiday, we can set one day a year aside to practice and celebrate family safety.

Family Safety Day happens on Spring Forward Day, the day we shift the clocks one hour later to begin Daylight Savings Time. My conspirators and I are making it a thing, starting in 2025. I hope you'll join us.

What Is Family Safety Day? Family Safety Day is a day we set aside to work on safety as a family. We arrange ahead with our work, our partners, and our children to make it all hands on deck. Everybody pitches in. Everybody spends time together. Everybody is safer at the end of the day.

A perfect family safety day combines multiple elements.

- Sleeping in, because sufficient sleep is important to all kinds of safety situations.
- Sharing a nutritious breakfast while talking about the plan for the day.
- Completing several small safety tasks, like replacing the batteries in the smoke detectors and filling up car tires to the proper pressure.

- Completing two or three moderate safety tasks, like restocking first aid kits, cleaning the car, or anchoring tall furniture to wall studs.
- Making progress on one major safety task, like research for an upcoming vacation or taking an online (or in-person) safety class.
- Reviewing and rehearsing one or more family safety plans.
- Placing an order for important safety equipment.
- Going out as a family while practicing awareness skills and safety games.
- Eating dinner together while debriefing the day's activities and lessons.

Done right, the whole day is fun and educational for everybody while also helping to make the family safer. Even better, parents lead by example the whole day by showing they prioritize safety.

That Magical Time of the Year. The key to a good Family Safety Day is not approaching it like a chore. The day is a time for families to play together, to learn from each other, and to celebrate how much they care about one another's safety.

It's an opportunity to celebrate successes, solve problems as a team, and learn new skills. As parents, we can make it fun while simultaneously making each activity teach the lessons we want our children to learn.

Family Safety Day happens on Spring Forward Day. Come to the website, or my Instagram or YouTube channel, to see what resources and activities I've set up for anybody who can participate. If you can, I invite you to join us.

If you can't do it on Spring Forward Day, commit to doing it some other day. The Family Safety Day spirit lives in us all year round.

16 Use the Phone Number Trick

One of the Golden Rules talked about how we should teach our children not to fear strangers but to know which strangers they should approach if they need help and can't find us. That's all well and good, but only the first step.

If our child gets separated and finds a safe adult, they must be able to help that adult find us. That's the next skill to teach our youngest children.

The phone is the easiest way for a helpful stranger to get in touch with us. They can call us, find a rendezvous point, and reunite us with our child. If we're unreachable, they can hand our children off to the police, who can use our number to find our address. Easy-peasy.

But only if our children know our phone numbers well enough to remember and repeat them under stress.

The best trick I know to teach this quickly is as simple as it is devious.

Every child in the modern age has a mobile device of preference where they watch silly shows and play their video games. This might be your phone, loaned out in key moments. It might be a tablet of their very own, or your old phone in a nice child-proof protective case. The specifics don't matter for this.

Whatever the device is, make its passcode your phone number.

They will have it memorized by the end of the day. Tell them what it is and why it's important for them to remember. Your child will know that number by heart, remember it under stress, and be able to repeat it no matter what.

Can We Be Honest for a Second? Some people will tell you that our children shouldn't have access to mobile devices until well after they're old enough to just know our phone numbers. Some of those people are qualified experts in developmental psychology and neuroscience. Buzzkills they may be, but they're probably right.

But come on.

I don't personally know any parents who follow that advice. I'm sure they exist, but they're rare. For the rest of us, it would be silly to avoid using this simple safety trick just out of some guilt we were made to feel by a mommy blogger who also cares deeply about GMOs and doesn't vaccinate her kids.

This method works and works well. Parents only need it during a brief window. If you're in that window, try it today.

17 Close the Bedroom Door

"Leave the door open, please."

It's a request almost every parent gets during one stage or another, or every stage, of the bedtime drama. Some of us say yes because it lets a little light into the room without keeping little ones awake.

Some of us say yes because it helps our children feel still connected to the home and family as they drift off to sleep. Some of us say yes because, apparently, an open door is the only way to keep monsters in the closet or under the bed.

Some of us say yes because it's easier than the argument and tears that come with saying no.

But we should say no.

When we say no in any circumstance, the next words out of most children's mouths is usually, "Why not?"

The Answers We Give. Let's be honest and admit that sometimes we fib to our kids. When we answer that question, we might give any kind of crazy answer ranging from the science of sleep, to helping them become individuals, to some sort of family mythology.

Don't feel bad. We all do it, and in the heat of the bedtime battle, anything that gets the light off and the door shut is fair game. What's right is what works.

The Real Answers. Even as we're telling our children about the sleep study we didn't read and probably made up, we know the real reasons we want that door closed. Reasons like:

- You want to watch a movie with scary content, and an open door means they'll hear all the gunfire, screams, and cussing.
- That little bit of light lets them read until way past when they should be asleep.
- A door open even a little bit gets taken as an invitation to keep coming out for yet one more hug, glass of water, or other ninja toddler sleep avoidance mission.
- Your child talks in their sleep, and honestly it gets a little spooky in the middle of the night.
- You intend to engage in sexy times with your co-parent and don't want the little one hearing it.

These reasons are perfectly valid, even if our kids aren't old enough to understand them. Even if we're not quite old enough to admit them to our kids.

Valid as they are, they're not the main reason to keep that bedroom door shut tight from their very first night sleeping in the nursery alone.

Your Final Answer. A closed door, even a cheap and hollow bedroom door, can hold back a fire by ten minutes or more. That's ten extra minutes for an older child to get into their shoes and out the window. That's ten extra minutes for you to come through the window to rescue an infant or toddler. In the worst-case scenario, that's ten extra minutes for rescue personnel to get in there and get your children out.

Take a minute and go to YouTube. Search for "closed door fire." You'll find a five-minute video titled "See the Dramatic Difference a Door Can Make," posted by the Fire Safety Research Institute. Watch the whole thing, or go to the reveal at 3:37. Or pick any of the shorter videos the search turns up.

The point is that closed bedroom door can save a life in a fire. Your child's life.

Those reasons above might apply or they might not, but shut the door for this one reason that matters most.

18 Safety Sweep the Yard

They say cleanliness is next to godliness. I don't know about that. A lot of research has found that smarter people have messier homes, desks, and lives.

What I do know is that cleanliness can help you avoid meeting any gods earlier than you'd prefer.

Here's What I Mean. Picture the average yard at a family home. I mean a real family home, the Monday after a holiday barbecue. Not a "family home" as pictured in a family magazine. That picture is going to include:

- Bikes and scooters left lying wherever
- Firestarter sitting on a picnic table
- A leftover trash bag in one corner, plus one for cans and bottles

- A garden hose left across a walking path
- Debris from trimming the hedge left in a pile

And all manner of other items. Every one of those things is a safety hazard. People can trip over stuff left in the yard. Chemicals get spilled or swallowed. That loose fence board can fall, exposing nails.

It gets worse.

Those are safety hazards to people engaged in everyday activities, the sorts of things families get up to during their normal routine. Now, imagine navigating the yard and paths in the middle of the night while escaping a fire. Or fleeing a home invader who just kicked in the door. Or while you're practicing a bug-out drill.

Safety Sweeping the Yard. For some families, cleaning the yard and paths around the home is a simple and easy process. They have everything squared away most of the time, so they just have to pick up a few stray items and they're good to go.

For the rest of us, the safety sweep is a project. Here's the best way I've encountered to make that project successful.

Step one is to walk around the house, scanning for three kinds of things:

- Items you keep someplace specific, but they aren't where they go
- Items out in the open that don't yet have a home
- Stationary hazards that need repair

Walk through and write down everything. If you're super-nerdy like me, use a map. Once you have your list, it's time to deal with each category.

Handling the first type is simple. Pick them up and put them where they go. Or have your kids do it. They're probably the reason the stuff is scattered all over in the first place.

The second type requires an extra step. First, decide where that item lives. That might require some rearrangement of other items, or a quick donation run with some stuff you don't need, or building some storage. Once that's done, the item in question no longer belongs in this category. It's an item that has a home, but isn't there.

Stationary hazards are things like holes that could turn an ankle, branches sticking out at forehead height, or fences that need replacement or repair. These get subdivided into two types:

- Things you can fix in five minutes or less. A branch you can trim back, or a nail sticking out of a fence board, are examples of this.
- Things you need extra time to fix or that require tools or supplies you don't have. Fixing a pothole or squaring a gate are examples of this kind of project.

The first category you just fix. Get the tools, take the time, and make it happen. For the others, order the equipment you need and schedule time in the near future to get it fixed.

When you've finished all three categories, you're all set. The yard is clear of hazards, safe to play in, and safe to move through during drills or true emergencies.

One last thing. I built a tool called the *Safe Home Blueprint*. It's a workbook for making your house safer and more secure, twenty-eight pages long. It walks you through this and other key safety tasks for your home. Because you bought this book, I'm happy to send you a copy at my cost. Just ping me and I'll get you set up.

19 Childproof Where You Don't Expect It

I learned a lot when we adopted our oldest son when he was seven years old. It was an in-family adoption based on a medical situation, so we went from zero kids to "Woah! We have a kid!" in just a couple of weeks.

Specifically, I learned a great deal about childproofing the home of two martial artists who also enjoy DIY projects.

I learned even more when our youngest was on his way. We had nine months of warning for that one, so we were better able to prepare. Still, when that baby became mobile we discovered so many lessons we had not yet learned.

I'm sharing those with you here so you can avoid those mistakes and go forth to make bold, creative, unique mistakes of your very own.

Cleat Up the Curtains. The cords that let us draw blinds and curtains in the house can be strangulation hazards, even for older kids who in theory can get untangled. The same goes for curtains in general. Even without strangulation, they can wrap around limbs and cut off circulation badly enough or long enough to do serious damage.

Buy cleats for less than a dollar each and mount them well out of reach, and maintain the habit of always using them. If you have the money, you can get cordless blinds that avoid the need for extra care.

Unplug Everything. Plugs offer two hazards for inquisitive hands and minds. Most obviously, they can get partially unplugged and become a shock hazard. They also turn any appliance into a falling hazard if little ones pull on them hard enough.

Fix this with two approaches. First, anything that doesn't need plugging in gets unplugged when not in use. That includes table lamps, televisions, computers, even medium appliances like the microwave. Large appliances like your fridge and stove need to remain plugged in, but the plug is behind the appliance so little ones aren't likely to reach the hazard.

Second, set up a way to corral and store those cords out of reach so they're no longer a falling hazard and can't strangle children like a curtain cleat.

Lose the Stuffies. Don't actually get rid of all the stuffies in the house. They've been demonstrated repeatedly as good for a child's mental health. However, babies, cruisers, and toddlers should not sleep with their stuffed animal friends. When they're too young, and not yet strong enough, stuffies can be a smothering hazard.

The safest cribs are empty except for the baby, their zip-up onesie jammies, and a firm mattress. If they're already very attached to a stuffie, you can put it within sight but out of reach to keep baby company through the night.

Close the Doors. In an earlier chapter, I go into detail about how a closed bedroom door can save a child from a fire. Closed doors also help with a long list of other safety issues. They keep kids out of bathrooms and away from slipping, drowning, and poisoning hazards. They let parents leave some rooms more cluttered, or as homes for more dangerous toys. They protect little ones from the dangers associated with most garages. Closing doors and maintaining the habit of keeping them closed is more important than it's natural to think.

As kids get older and learn to open doors on their own, we can extend this by installing those knob cuffs. By the time our children grow large and strong enough to navigate through those, they're of an age where they can understand dangers and start avoiding them on their own.

Save a Toilet Paper Tube. Choking sends 12,000 children to the emergency room every year. About 4,000 of them don't come home. Part of why it's so prevalent is that children can choke on surprisingly large, and surprisingly small, objects. On the small end of the range, assume anything larger in diameter than their pinky finger is wide enough to choke on.

For the large end, keep a toilet paper tube handy. Anything that can slide through it is small enough to go down part of a baby's windpipe. It's a handy test for food, toys, game components, tools, or anything else that might fall victim to the hand-to-mouth lifestyle of young ones. If an object fits, it sits out of reach.

Store Tablecloths and Doilies. Tablecloths and doilies make furniture more attractive, and keep it attractive by protecting it from the slings and arrows (and cat claws and magic markers) of family life. The trouble is, those overhanging bits of cloth often drape within reach of children. Especially for cruisers and toddlers, who might reach toward them for support, you're already imagining the worst that can happen.

Until the children are tall enough to see over the table, put the tablecloths and doilies away. They're more risk than they're worth.

20 Upgrade Your Medical Training

I know, I know. Kickpunchery and range time are so much more fun than a first-aid class. I agree.

As parents, though, how many times in the last five years have you had to physically defend yourself? Compare that to how many times you've had to administer any kind of first aid.

Unless you have a specialized job or some seriously questionable decision-making, there's no comparison. Medical training and experience will come up far more often than self-defense skills. It pays to keep them sharp.

Not only that, it's also a never-ending opportunity to gain new, useful, interesting skills. No matter how good you are, there's always another level.

Starting Out. Depending on who you ask, just over or just under one-third of adults in America have received basic first-aid training. That means two-thirds of us haven't.

If you haven't, find a first-aid/CPR/AED class through the Red Cross or your local Community Education or Parks and Rec department. It will take about a day, and cost less than fifty dollars. You will come out much better prepared than you went in.

If you have, ask how long it's been since you took a refresher. A lot of us got that certification for a job years ago and haven't thought about it since. Depending on your situation, you might get what you need from reviewing some videos online. If it's been a while, though, taking the full class is always an option.

For example, most of my high school and college jobs required first-aid certification. I re-upped them every couple of years until I was almost thirty. Then I had a ten-year gap where I figured I had it down. I went to get it again for a part-time gig and found out they'd changed how to do CPR. *And* they'd added using AED devices.

You never know.

The Next Level. For people with basic first-aid training or experience, I highly recommend the Stop the Bleed program. It's exactly what it sounds like: a quick course on how to manage serious bleeding to keep somebody alive until the professionals show up.

The program is free and effective. In some areas, you can find in-person sessions with a Google search. They have an online option if there's nobody near you.

Getting Up There. The next stage will depend on what you realistically think you'll encounter, or what you think will be most interesting and fun. At this level, many of the skills overlap so no course's information will be wasted.

Some of the better options include:

- Getting instructor certifications for training you've already received
- Training specific to the ages, medical needs, or activities of people in your family
- Emergency trauma medicine training for better accident response
- Wilderness medicine, which teaches you how to treat somebody when an ambulance can't get there
- Tactical medical courses, which combine first aid with self-defense. This kind of training is for scenarios that are not very likely to occur, but it can be very fun.

Another nice thing about this stage is you can get new information, or different angles on the same skills, from different courses year after year.

Going Pro. If you want to dive even deeper, consider professional-level courses. You don't have to change careers, but with enough time and money you can complete an LPN or EMT course over the course of a few years.

Volunteering with local search and rescue, hospitals, law enforcement, or fire can also work. You'll be giving back to your community while receiving excellent training and applicable experience.

These options are time consuming and can cost a lot of money, but if you have enough of both they can make you ready for almost anything.

Wherever You Go, There You Are. Begin this process with an honest self-assessment of your medical skills, experience, and knowledge. One thing that makes this challenging is how much bad information is out there and how often we can't know what we don't know.

One way to start is to hop online and watch a few introductory first-aid tutorials. You will pretty quickly see how much you already knew versus how much you didn't know or had wrong.

From that grounding, figure out where you want to go.

Fire and Accident Prevention Action Plan

General advice doesn't do much good, especially for people with free time as limited as active parents. Here's a quick checklist of the most vital action items you can start with today about fire and accident prevention.

Do these this week and you're on your way to a safer family:

- ❏ Move any medications and poisons out of reach and behind locks.
- ❏ Choose a specific safe place as your default morning coffee or tea spot.
- ❏ Set your child's device password to match your phone number.

Find an hour soon and take action to become even safer:

- ❏ Look up the recommended number and placement of smoke detectors, fire extinguishers, and carbon monoxide detectors for a home with your size and layout. If necessary, order new equipment or move what you have.
- ❏ Shift to a policy of closing bedroom doors at night, and do whatever is necessary to get little ones on board with the change.
- ❏ Meet a first responder you know for coffee or lunch and "pick their brains" about your safety situation.

Make time for these important long-term projects to become the safest family on your block:

- ❏ Set up and perform your own Family Safety Day!
- ❏ Safety sweep your yard, and make any repairs or upgrades you find necessary.
- ❏ Sign up for and complete the next level of your medical training.

SECTION 3

CAR AND DRIVING SAFETY

Introduction by Jason Hoschouer

Jason Hoschouer is a retired law enforcement officer with twenty-three years of experience. His specialty was traffic enforcement, having spent half his career assigned to the Traffic Division as a Motor Officer. He also has over six-hundred hours of collision-specific investigations training and is a POST-certified Master Instructor. Find him at the What's Your Emergency *podcast.*

As a retired motor officer and former lead investigator for my department's Fatal Collision Reconstruction team, I can firmly state I know a thing or two about vehicle safety.

Preparing for bad things has a weird superpower of keeping those bad things at bay. All too often, it's unprepared drivers who find themselves in that briny pickle juice situation without a solution at hand. This chapter lays out simple, affordable, easily implemented ideas to keep Murphy as far away from you and those you care about.

Listen, some of the guidance herein is obvious. Drinking and driving = bad. We're all agreed, right? Sometimes, however, even unbeknownst to the driver, their perfectly acceptable prescription meds may interact adversely with something else that would otherwise not be considered an issue. It's the combination that sneaks up on you. The advice about being aware of drug interactions is worth its weight in mangled steel.

21 Clean Your Car

Not everything we do to keep our family safe is exciting. I know, I'm disappointed, too. I've been a dad for more than twenty years, and at no point has a squad of ninja biker pirate zombies attacked us in the car.

Yes, it's fun to take an evasive/defensive driving course where we get to learn bootleg turns and high-speed maneuvers.

Yes, it scratches a certain itch to get to the range or on the mat and practice self-defense.

Yes, it's gratifying to stock our cars for serious emergencies with all kinds of comforting and nifty gear.

No, none of that helps protect our families against the most common causes of injury when we're on the road. Do you know what will do that?

As the title suggests, cleaning our car.

Wait, What? Why? For a lot of reasons, starting with the most dramatic. If you get into an accident, your car stops, but everything in the car maintains forward momentum. That's why seat belts and air bags save lives.

Loose items in your car don't have seatbelts. They fly around and can hit your family members hard enough to injure or kill them.

If you're old enough to be a parent, you're probably old enough to have experienced a lesser illustration of this in action. Remember what happened to your cassettes or CDs when you took a corner too hard? It's like that, only more like a tree branch in a hurricane.

Car Cleaning Safety Checklist. That's the most dramatic reason, but there are plenty more. The easiest way to describe them is to list the things we should clean on a regular basis, along with why they're important.

From front to back:

- Polish the headlight covers so they illuminate farther and better.
- Clean your windshield, other windows, and mirrors to maximize visibility.

- Clear everything off your dashboard, including anything you've intentionally glued or affixed there.
- Clean off your center console and glove box. Clean out anything not vital, and store all your vital stuff inside.
- Remove any detritus from the foot well in the driver's seat. It can interfere with your ability to use pedals. The other foot wells are a good idea but not critical.
- Clean up everything in and around the back seat. The few items you need in the car can go in the center console or back-of-seat storage.

If you drive a minivan or SUV, also secure anything in that back area that would be a trunk on a regular car. There's enough clearance above the back seats that things can fly all the way forward in a crash.

If you have a pickup, make sure medium-size, medium-weight objects are similarly secured. The smallest objects won't penetrate the back window, and the heaviest won't move in a crash. But those things in the middle, like tool boxes or spare tires, can come through the back of the truck and hit your family.

While You're in There. Cleaning your car is one step toward car safety. Maintaining your car is another. It's a good idea to create a schedule of car care to make sure your vehicle is always as safe and reliable as possible.

Use your manufacturer's recommended maintenance as the skeleton, then add switching out the wipers, checking and topping off fluids, checking tire treads, inflating tires, and rotating emergency supplies to the list.

This can be especially powerful if you know (or learn) how to do each of these tasks yourself. Involve your kids as they get old enough so that by the time they're grown they're fully prepared for the job.

22 Lock in by 10

We already know better than to drive drunk, or high, or exhausted, or compromised in any of the dozens of other ways that impact how safe we are behind the wheel. We're already teaching our kids not to drive drunk. For those of driving age, we repeat the instruction in so many words. For the younger ones, we teach by example when we only have water at dinner, use a designated driver, or call an Uber to get home from a party.

That's as it should be, but it's not the complete story.

It's not complete because we share the roads with irresponsible people who do drive drunk, high, exhausted, distracted, or otherwise impaired.

According to the National Highway Traffic Safety Administration, the days of the year with the most drunk drivers are New Year's Eve, Christmas Eve, Christmas, Thanksgiving, Independence Day, Memorial Day, and the Friday after Thanksgiving. Halloween and Superbowl Sunday are also high-risk nights.

On those nights, consider setting the rule that wherever your children are at 10 pm is where they will wake up in the morning. This keeps them off the roads during those most dangerous hours. If you follow the same rule for yourself, it doesn't just keep you safer. It also means you can indulge a little more yourself, since you'll be bunking in as well.

This can feel like an extreme measure, and most nights it will be erring on the side of caution. It's probably unnecessary if you live in a walkable neighborhood with good pedestrian protection. If the route home is along an undivided rural highway, though, this might be essential.

Buzzed Driving. I don't know many adults who drink and have never driven home while a little impaired. Not enough to be breaking the law, but enough to be operating below 100 percent. I have been guilty of it myself but stopped after hearing one way to look at it.

If I have one beer with dinner, I might get behind the wheel at 95 percent of my abilities. With actual drunk drivers on the road, somebody else could put me in a position where that extra 5 percent could save my family's life.

23 Keep Your Old Shoes

I stole this hack wholesale from Nick Hughes in his astonishingly useful book *How to Be Your Own Bodyguard*, which I had the privilege of beta reading and helping edit for its most recent edition. It's simple to write, to read, to understand, and to implement. Ready? Here it is.

Keep your second-newest pair of running shoes or hiking shoes in your trunk, with a pair of good socks rolled up inside.

With those babies on board, you always have a pair of good, broken-in footwear to change into if your car breaks down or gets stuck.

Because Murphy's Law is real, it seems like we never get stuck wearing our best all-weather gear and most comfortable shoes. It happens on date night, with high heels on one set of feet and wingtips on the other. Walking for help is difficult enough, and this small bit of preparation means it's not more difficult than it has to be.

This is a little trickier to do for our kids, since we usually only buy new shoes when they outgrow the old ones. A pair of crocs or slightly oversized rain boots can do the trick for them nicely, though.

Like I said, this hack was simple to write. It's so simple to read and understand that you've already done so. Implementation will take you five minutes if you have some old shoes and good socks in the house. If you don't, just remember this when you replace the sneakers you have on right now.

24 Stop Where You Can See Tires

This is another short, simple trick used by bodyguards from all over the world that you can turn into an everyday habit to keep you safe from all kinds of danger.

When you stop in traffic…

…always stop far enough away from the car in front of you that you can see their back tires. That's the whole tire, from its top to where it touches the road. Being that far from the car in front of you means you have enough space to turn hard and get out of that lane of traffic.

The "tacticool" operator crowd will tell you that's so your car has someplace to go if a carjacker or mugger approaches you. That's true, but it's not the whole reason to do this. Some other reasons this is a good idea include:

- If you get rear-ended, your car is less likely to skid into the vehicle in front of it.
- In gridlock, you have more options to get into less stuck traffic.
- If you have a medical emergency in your car, this lets you weave into faster-moving lanes or onto the shoulder.
- If the car ahead of you breaks down or otherwise gets stuck, you can move around it more quickly.

Although this rule is helpful, it doesn't do much good in the center lane. You can't turn hard and move over if there's no space to the left or the right.

If you feel the need for that extra mobility for any reason, drive in an outside lane. That way there's always space to go if you need to. If you're stuck in an inside lane, still follow this rule. That way, when an opening appears in another lane, you'll be able to drive into it.

While We're Talking About Distance. Staying far enough back isn't just for when your car is stopped.

You might remember from your driving manual that we're supposed to stay about three car lengths behind the vehicle in front of us (in some states, it calls for a count of three between that car passing a fixed point and our car doing the same). Either way, it's in the manual for a reason.

It's probably an overstatement for most cars, especially since brakes and tires keep getting better, but the rule has stayed the same for more than fifty years. But really, if we're going to err… we should err on the side of safety when it comes to our kids.

Bottom line when moving and when stopped: stay far enough back to own your safety and that of everybody else in the car.

25 Install a Dash Cam

Research by the National Surface Transportation Safety Center for Excellence has found that dash cams in cars can cut accidents in half. As of this writing, most of that research involves commercial fleets rather than family cars, but that number is significant enough to get my attention.

Sure, there's a part of me that rails against putting cameras in my cars. But that's the part still reeling from reading *1984* at a formative age. It's not the part responsible for making sure my kids survive high school and early adulthood.

Dash cams are unmitigatedly good for driving safety. They improve driver accountability by recording what happened. They record the behavior of other drivers, which can reduce incidents of road rage and police misconduct.

With teens, some surveys have found that just having one on board calms down risky behavior. It's like having you in the car with them at all times.

Clearly, dash cams make cars safer. Let's talk about all three kinds.

Forward Dash Cams. As the name implies, these cameras are mounted on the dashboard and aimed out through the windshield and over the hood. They're what you see most often in YouTube dashcam videos, recording the motions of the car and what's happening around it.

These are most popular among commercial fleets and with people in regions with high crime or police corruption. Their main job is to record what happens to the car, and they improve safety in those areas.

Interior Dash Cams. Mounted high on the windshield, on the dash, or on your rearview mirror, these cameras monitor the interior of the car. Their job is to record what happens *in* the car.

As you might imagine, these cameras have the strongest impact on risky behaviors among teen drivers. The front-facing models can tell you about speed, tailgating, and similar choices. These will tell you if your teen is texting while driving, or their buddy in the passenger seat is punching them in the arm.

Models with both front and interior (sometimes called front and rear) cameras are common and cost on average $40 to $60 more than single-direction options.

Performance Monitors. If you want some benefits of dash cams but just can't go so far as to install video surveillance in the car, this is a less intrusive option.

When you take a modern car to the mechanic, they plug a cable into a receptacle back behind and under the steering column. That cable connects their computer to a computer in the car, sharing all kinds of information about how the car has been driven.

Small boxes the size of a notary stamp are available, which record the data in real time and send it to a designated person. You might have seen one as an offer from your insurance company, where they monitor your driving habits and give you a discount if the data qualifies you. Newer models attach via Bluetooth to the car and the phone.

You can get one to install, then gather the data on your phone. It's not as complete, easy to access, or easily referenced in conversation, but it's better than nothing for people who don't want an actual camera.

For Two Wheels. Let's start with the near-unanimous opinion of every driving safety teacher, motor officer, insurance adjustor, ER nurse, reconstructive surgeon, public health expert, and loan officer I've asked about this.

Don't let teenagers drive motorcycles.

They're barely ready to navigate the roads while surrounded by half a ton of steel equipped with multiple safety features. We're not doing our job as protectors sending them out there with just their jacket and a helmet.

But if you must let them, a GoPro-style camera on a head mount does the job of the dash cams I've just mentioned. The numbers aren't as dramatic, but they're still an improvement.

26 Put Your Phone in the Back Seat

Every year, we see an article about how a baby or toddler died because a parent left them in the car on a hot day. Every year, somebody on the news suggests putting the phone in the back seat so there's something important there to grab and remind us there's a baby back there too.

When that advice comes down, we see a stream of memes that poke fun because what kind of parent will remember their phone but not their kid? What is wrong with their priorities?

You might be nodding right now. Parents who need a reminder about having their kid in the car deserve at least some spirited mockery.

But Here's the Thing. Most incidents like this do not involve a drunk, reckless, irresponsible parent making a tragically stupid mistake.

The overwhelming majority happen with a parent whose usual morning routine doesn't include dropping the little one off at day care. That adult is suddenly up for that duty, and autopilot exists.

Autopilot is especially powerful in the fog of early parent sleep deprivation. The parent goes through their morning routine and forgets about the child in the back. If that child falls asleep in the car, as many do, the worst can happen.

That means we're all vulnerable here. Even smart, dedicated, safe parents fall victim to autopilot. If I asked every reader of this book to count back to the last time they got home in the car with little to no memory of the drive, very few could make it even a week.

It's Not About What's Important. It's about what's *automatic.* The joke suggests that some parents' phones are more important to them than their children. That's nonsense. Mean-spirited nonsense, if we're being honest.

Our cell phones are an automatic part of our day. We get to work, we reach automatically for where the phone usually is, and it's not there. We say, "Huh, that's funny…"

And we remember why it's not there. We look into the back seat and see our sleeping child. We start to cuss because we'll be late for work now, and we start to cry because of what could have happened.

Cussing and crying are way better than the alternative.

With kids of that age, we can 100 percent prevent that tragedy in every situation by simply putting our phones in the back seat as an automatic habit. Every time we go back there to get it, we see what else is back there.

To say nothing about how much harder it is to text and drive with it back there.

27 Crash Your Car

You've seen this in movies and television hundreds of times. A bad guy gets in the car with a victim and threatens them, forcing them to drive someplace.

Back in the Golden Rules section, we talked about Crime Scene #2 and why you should never go with a criminal who tries to move you. The advice there covered a situation where you were approached in public.

But what about if you're already in the car? Your mobility is compromised by a seat belt, the doors, and the fact that you're sitting down. Your kids are strapped in behind you, maybe in child seats that take a minute or more to get them out of. You're already in the best tool for taking people to Crime Scene #2.

It's a bad situation, so what do you do about it?

Crash It! Immediately crash the car.

If you're driving, wrench the wheel and hit something. If you're in another seat, leap across and grab the steering wheel...or just attack the bad guy in the driver's seat. Go for their eyes and don't stop until the car crashes.

Do not waste time. Do not wait for the car to get up to lethal crashing speeds. Ram the nearest solid object. This is the best advice for three reasons.

First, it resets the physical situation. Whatever body positions everyone was in before the crash get jostled around and change. Since you're expecting it, you will be in a position to retake control and make an effective counterattack.

Second, it makes a lot of noise and gathers lots of attention. That old saw about yelling "Fire" instead of "Help" turned out to not be true, but it is true that people pay attention to car crashes. They look out windows, whip out cell phones, and come running to help.

Third, the combination of the first two put immense pressure on the criminal to escape. His plan has gone wrong, he's probably hurt, and people are starting to pay attention. To carry out his intentions, he has to get a new vehicle and somehow bring you with him. In most cases, he will just try to flee.

Won't I Get Hurt? Maybe. It depends on how fast you were going. You will definitely get hurt less than what the criminal had in mind for you when you got where he was going. Your kids are strapped in, so they're unlikely to get too badly hurt if you crash it before reaching highway speeds.

Will the criminal hurt you in retaliation? That's a possibility, but first he won't have the time or privacy to hurt you the way he would at Crime Scene #2.

Second, he's compromised and surprised. You have a much better chance at an effective counterattack.

You can also take some steps just before the crash to help you come out less injured. Close your teeth with your tongue behind them. Tuck your chin like a boxer. Relax to the degree relaxing is possible in circumstances like this. All of that will minimize damage in a minor auto collision.

28 Watch Out for Drug Interactions

By now, we know better than to drive drunk. As I said earlier, driving buzzed isn't great either because the 5-percent impairment from a glass of beer might be the 5 percent you needed to turn that crash into a near miss.

Another important thing to consider, that's much less well known, comes from a traffic enforcement officer I've known for a while.

It starts with remembering why the crime is no longer DWI, Driving While Intoxicated. It's DUI, Driving Under the Influence, or keeping DWI but making it Driving While Impaired. In both cases, they're expanding the definition of driving when you shouldn't to include more things than alcohol.

This officer reports that at least half of the DUI arrests he has to make aren't from alcohol. They're not from drugs. They're from drug interactions.

A combination of two or more drugs (which can include alcohol and caffeine) sometimes has a synergistic effect. An example of this is how effective a few painkillers or prescription sleep aids and some hard liquor is as a tool for suicide. Neither the drug, nor the alcohol, could do it alone in those doses…but together they're deadly.

In this case, a normal amount of prescription painkiller taken before breakfast can combine with one glass of wine with lunch and put your driving well within the scope of a DUI conviction.

Some interactions of prescription drugs with each other, or in rare cases with certain foods, can be harmful or even lethal.

Two websites, rxlist.com and drugs.com, offer drug interaction checkers that laypeople can easily understand. They're an excellent starting point for finding out how your prescriptions work and play well with others.

It's also smart to bring a list of what you're taking and to ask about alcohol or other recreational drugs when you go to pick up new prescriptions. Pharmacists are trained to look for this exact thing. They have a not-particularly-funny joke amongst themselves about how their primary job is to "keep doctors from killing their patients."

29 Store Your Camping Gear in Your Trunk

Lots of families go camping once a year or so. Most should. Camping gives families quality time together and helps us all appreciate little conveniences like running water and clean clothes. There's also a raft of evidence suggesting time outdoors is good for our mental and physical health.

But that's not why I'm bringing camping up here.

One drawback of camping is all the gear. You need a tent, sleeping bags and pads for each family member, a camp stove, some water storage, a first-aid kit, and odds and ends like camping cookware, rope, basic tools, and fire-starting equipment.

That takes up room in the house. Maybe a corner of the closet. Maybe a few tubs in the garage. Maybe some space in the shed.

It's not much room, but it is room you could be using for other things.

Which is the second most important reason to keep it in your car. So what's the first reason?

What Is Camping Gear? Let's look at that list again: tent, sleeping bags and pads, camp stove, water storage, medical supplies, cookware, rope, tools, and fire-starting equipment.

In other words: shelter, warmth, food, water, fire, and basic tools. The things you need on hand in an emergency. If you keep them in your backpack, they're even in an easily portable container.

Kept in the car, stored camping gear becomes an ideal bug-out bag ready and waiting for any emergency. It also contains most of what you'll need if your car breaks down and you can't summon help right away.

It Gets Even Better. The camping gear isn't just emergency equipment. It's emergency equipment you're already familiar with. You'll never be struggling with the instruction manual as the stuff hits the fan.

It's already in the car. If an emergency calls for you to hit the road, you just get in and go. If you're sheltering in place, you know where the gear is. Since you drive your car to most places you go, the gear is on hand if an emergency strikes when you're not at home.

This plan also costs less. You don't have to buy camping gear *and* a bug-out kit. They multitask.

One Last Little Thing. Put some maps in there. They aren't necessary when you go car camping or hiking with the family, but if things get really sketchy you can't rely on GPS.

I recommend putting in a map of your city, a map of your county, and one of your state. When you travel, pick up a map of that area, too. Use it to teach your kids how to read and work with maps on paper, then store the ones you think might be relevant later on.

30 Build a Car Emergency Kit

When I began to focus on learning about family safety, I found out my emergency kit game was both a weak point and an easy place to begin.

Part of my efforts to fix that was interviewing a representative from AAA, who happily walked me through what they recommend a fully stocked car emergency kit should include. I'm sharing it with you here.

The Purpose of an Emergency Kit. Despite its name, a car emergency kit's primary purpose is to prevent inconveniences from becoming emergencies. For example, not having snow tires or chains can mean you're stuck in the snow for a few hours. Having the right traction gear means you just drive slower for a while.

They also prevent emergencies from becoming tragedies. If your car gets stuck in a winter storm, having gloves, a coat, and a space blanket mean nobody's freezing to death.

Components of a Car Emergency Kit. Although each vehicle and family is different, here is what AAA recommends we put in every car.

- Jumper cables
- Inflated, functional spare tire
- Tire change kit
- Snow chains, or those new tire bootie things
- A waterproof tarp
- Work gloves
- One-gallon bag of sand or cat litter

- Folding shovel or entrenching tool
- A car tool kit that matches your repair skills
- Three or four shop rags
- Duct tape
- Ice scraper
- Car escape tool
- Road flares, signal triangle, or LED flares
- Flashlight
- Glowsticks, one for every family member
- Hand crank radio/charger/flashlight
- Spare batteries for all devices
- First-aid kit
- Mylar emergency blankets
- Spare comfortable shoes for each family member
- Weather-appropriate gear for each family member
- One or two days worth of emergency food
- One gallon of water for each seat in the car
- Comfort items to alleviate boredom and reassure children

The Most Important Tool. Nothing on the list does anybody good if they don't know how to use them.

The good news is a lot of it is intuitive, or something we do so often we don't need training. We all know how to put on a coat and gloves before going out in the snow.

Other things, like the specific chains for our current car or those new LED flares, require training or a refresher. YouTube is full of videos, often from the manufacturer, to watch and practice along with and develop those skills.

A third category is the most dangerous: things we think we know how to use but aren't sure. Not all cars jump the same way anymore, for instance, and car escape tools don't work on all forms of tempered glass. In the middle of a crisis is not the best time to find those things out.

Best advice: go through the list. Check off everything you are 100-percent certain you know how to use. For everything else, even what you're 99-percent on, jump on YouTube and make sure.

Car and Driving Safety Action Plan

General advice doesn't do much good, especially for people with free time as limited as active parents. Here's a quick checklist of the most vital action items you can start with today about car and driving safety.

Do these this week and you're on your way to a safer family:

- ❑ Find an old pair of shoes for each family member and put them in your car.
- ❑ Take your camping gear and put it in your trunk.
- ❑ Choose an out of reach spot in your car as your phone's new default resting space.

Find an hour soon and take action to become even safer:

- ❑ Thoroughly clean your car to remove potentially flying debris.
- ❑ Order online everything you need to complete your car emergency kit.
- ❑ Use drugs.com to research interactions for any medications your family uses.

Make time for these important long-term projects to become the safest family on your block:

- ❑ Order and install any equipment you need to keep your car clean and organized.
- ❑ Build the habit of stopping your car in traffic where you can still see the tires of the car in front of you.
- ❑ Research the best kind of dash cam for your car, order it, and install it.

SECTION 4

SAFETY AT SCHOOL

Introduction by Alain Burrese

Alain Burrese, JD, is the author of numerous books and video programs, and the Director of Training for Reflex Protect, a company that provides training and defensive products for law enforcement and civilians. Find him at surviveashooting.com and enjoylifesafely.com.

Active Shooter Incidents have steadily increased over the last couple of decades. It's the reason I wrote *Survive a Shooting*, and it is why I am paid to travel around the country helping organizations become better prepared with what they can do before, during, and after such terrible events.

While active shooter incidents are a legitimate threat to schools in these times we live in, there are other threats to our children's safety that are much more common and likely. Threats such as bullying, how children get to and from school, places kids go that are not as safe, and weather emergencies.

Fortunately, Jason addresses all these areas with actionable steps you can take to keep your children safer, including one of the most important things you can do to positively impact the safety of your children at school.

Keeping our children safe and raising them to become responsible adults are two of our greatest responsibilities. I thank Jason for providing guidance on how to do them better.

31 Stop Bullying by Being a Pain in the Butt

When parents come to me with questions about school safety, the most common questions have to do with bullying. It's a too-common problem and so complex I could do a whole book of its own on how to manage it.

For now, I want to cover a top-level piece of information most bullying advice doesn't cover: if your child is being bullied continuously, that only happens because an adult at school responsible for their safety isn't doing their job.

Teachers, staff, and administrators are responsible for keeping your child safe. Sometimes they don't. I want to emphasize that this is almost always because they're understaffed, underfunded, and undertrained. They have other, more urgent things pulling on their time when your child is being bullied.

They want to protect your child, but for some reason they can't in that moment.

Your First Line of Defense. When the adults in your child's school fail to keep them safe, the best thing to do is to make *not* doing that part of their job less convenient than doing it.

Again, they don't fail to stop bullying because they like bullies. They fail because they have packed schedules full of other important things. If you make your child's bullying issue fill up enough time and effort, they will reprioritize and help your child.

Very often, a quick word from you will do the trick. You let them know the situation is serious enough that your child told you about it, and that you've taken an interest. It boosts the level of urgency and the teacher or staffer gets on the case.

Start there. Ask your child if things have gotten better. A week later, send an email or make a phone call to either say thank you or ask about a better plan.

The response to that follow-up will tell you most of what you need to know. A teacher or staff member who is serious about your child's safety will engage wholeheartedly. One focused on other things will give that away in how they respond.

If the latter, it's time to step up your efforts.

The Next Level. If that follow-up leaves you unsatisfied, it's time to increase how inconvenient your child's bullying problem is for that teacher or staffer.

Begin by scheduling an after-school meeting with them, and invite the next person up the hierarchy. If it's with faculty, invite your child's teacher. If it's the teacher, invite the principal or department head. If it's the principal, find out who their direct report is at the district level.

The meeting alone can often do the trick. That happens during their prep and grading time, meaning it costs them personal time at the end of the school day. If you schedule one meeting, you imply that you're willing to schedule more.

During the meeting, lay out the exact issue and ask them for solutions. Critique and offer your own ideas. Do not leave the meeting until there is an agreed-upon plan with specific duties for all adults involved, and a timeline.

By showing that you will take up their time, you make your child's bullying problem a priority to the people who should have prioritized it before.

If That Doesn't Work. Sometimes that meeting doesn't work. You feel in the meeting that nobody is taking the situation seriously, or they refuse to book the meeting in the first place.

Whatever the reasons, if that happens it's time to escalate. Start with a meeting just with the superior you invited to the first one. If that doesn't work, contact the next person up in the district hierarchy. Set it all up via email, so you have a written record of everything.

While you're working your way through this, CC the principal and teacher on every email you send. It shows them you will not go away until the problem does.

If nothing happens at the district level, show up at a school board meeting. If the school board does nothing, talk to the press and even a lawyer.

Keep at it. Eventually you will reach a level of stakes and inconvenience that motivates the adults to do their jobs.

Always Remember. This chapter is coming off as pretty harsh about teachers. It's not meant to be. Most of the time you won't be dealing with irresponsible or uncaring people. You will be dealing with people who care very much but aren't given the time or tools to care properly for your child.

Stay compassionate and understanding, but also implacable. We can be aware of the massive challenges faced by teachers while still insisting our children be kept safe at school.

32 Don't Use a Pick-Up Code

Imagine a situation where you would normally pick up your child, or an emergency means you have to pick them up unexpectedly. Now, imagine something going so wrong that you can't go get them. You have to send somebody your child doesn't know or doesn't know well.

Now, you've already taught your child not to get in vehicles with people they don't know and trust. How can you communicate to them that this is an exception, and perfectly okay?

You have a codeword. Something like "Purple" or "Big Bird." My partner's family had the word "Pots," because it's "Stop" spelled backward and nearby signage might provide a visual reminder. Some families use a question-answer code where they teach their child to use something not unlike your bank's security questions.

If somebody offers your child a ride and provides the code, your child knows they're safe to get in the car with. If they can't provide it, your child knows to go immediately to a trusted adult and get help.

Pretty cool, right?

Code words can be a powerful part of your family safety plan in some situations. I use them with my partner and children. But pickup codes are a bad idea. We don't use them at all.

I get a lot of pushback on this, because it's something we were taught back in the day. It makes sense on the surface, and it feels gratifyingly tactical. But, like with other forms of bad advice, I learned better by listening to people who saw what happened when people relied on it.

What's Wrong with It? There are a lot of problems with this plan, the first of which is that it's not age appropriate. Younger children can't remember information that complex under the sort of stress that would cause this situation.

Study after study has shown this. They either forget to ask or get easily sidetracked and lured into the car. By the time a child's brain has developed enough to effectively use this technique, they're in their mid to late teens and can manage their own ride home.

Even if they don't get fooled, picture the physical process of exchanging a code word. How close will a child be standing to the adult, talking about something they've been told is a secret? They're likely to be whispering, which means they're within grabbing range of somebody who means them harm.

Add to this that the overwhelming majority of harm to children doesn't come from strangers. It comes from people they know, people who are close to the family and the child. People they trust. In short, people who are likely to be in on the code word, or able to get it by asking questions over a period of time.

Put all of that together, and it's easy to see how this is different from family emergency code words. The good ones are parent-directed and used in simple contexts. This is child-directed and used in complex situations.

What To Do Instead. The solution to this is so simple it's almost counterintuitive. It consists of two steps:

- **Step One**: Make a short list of people who can pick up your child. Have your child memorize it, and share the list with those in charge anywhere you leave them.
- **Step Two**: Never send anybody who's not on the list to pick up your child.

But wait a minute! What if you have to send somebody who's not on that list? Isn't the whole code word thing here specifically for that kind of emergency?

Imagine the situations where neither you, your partner, nor your one to three backups could go pick up your child. Those will be few and far between, but in most cases, where your child is will be safe and comfortable enough for the interim, and they'll be with adults you know you can trust.

Think about the locations where you drop off and pick up your children: school, day care, piano lessons, soccer practice, a friend's house. Which of those locations would abandon your child in a serious emergency or if your day blew up and you needed to be an hour late? How many of those locations are full of adults and playmates your child enjoys spending time with? How many of them aren't outfitted better than your home and mine with emergency supplies and facilities?

This solution is simple enough for even young children to remember. It's easy to share with other adults responsible for your kids. It's the better option.

33 Stop the Principal

One major challenge with keeping our kids safe at school is that we don't know what's going on there every day. Even if we volunteer regularly, we only see the school through that window.

Another challenge is that our kids are, as they say in literature classes, unreliable narrators. Sometimes they fib outright. Most of the time their perspective is incomplete. Either way, what they tell us is rarely the truth, the whole truth, and nothing but the truth.

At any given school, most of the time the principal has the most complete picture of what's going on. That picture is colored by their own biases and limitations, but they have access to the most information.

If You Have a Problem... Have a short, informal chat with the principal. Just a stand-up talk after school. Tell them what you're concerned about, but don't just listen to the reply.

Instead, carefully watch their facial expression as they hear what you have to say.

The principal knows what's going on in their school, so try to gauge whether or not you've surprised them.

For example, if your child tells you Johnny Johnson was mean to them on the playground, you mention this to the principal. If he gets an "oh, no, not again" face, you know Johnny Johnson is a bully and needs to be dealt with accordingly.

If the principal looks surprised, you know it's time to explore the matter more deeply with your child. Maybe Johnny had a bad day and the problem won't continue. Or maybe your kid misunderstood.

In all of these cases, you have more to work with than you did before that short chat with the principal.

Not Just for Kids. The same is true if you have an issue with a teacher or other member of the school staff. The principal knows which teachers are solid, which are close to retirement and phoning it in, and which are well-intentioned but new and still struggling. They know which are better matches for certain children and which aren't.

Look for surprise, or lack of it, when you mention your concern, and then you'll know better how to handle it.

If your issue is with the principal, use the same method with their direct report at the district level. That person, whatever their title, knows what's what with the principal under their supervision.

34 Watch the Bus Ramp

I want to start this by saying something most of us already know. The overwhelming majority of teachers and school administrators are dedicated professionals who love our children and want what's best for them.

However, they are dedicated and loving professionals with job duties that take up somewhere between 130 percent and

200 percent of the resources available to them. Their time, training, and support from the district are far less than what's ideal. It's frankly a miracle they accomplish what they do. When it comes to safety, most failures from teachers are because their minds and attention are being pulled in too many directions and once.

There are some teachers who are focused on things other than our kids' safety. Sometimes that's a temporary situation. Teachers are human, and sometimes they have personal crises on their minds. Sometimes it's a permanent part of their approach to the job.

Other times there's a safety problem in an entire school. The building has a culture of focus on things other than student safety. This happens for a variety of reasons and is extremely rare, but such schools do exist.

All of the above are possibilities about how serious the people caring for our children throughout the school day are about their safety. The trick is figuring out which one is going on at your school.

You figure it out by watching the bus ramp.

Twice a day, the bus ramp fills with large vehicles, smaller vehicles, bicycles, scooters, parents, teachers, and dozens of children. It's chaos in action, with higher stakes and more dangers than any other part of the school day. If school staff will be fully focused on student safety at any time, it should be mornings and afternoons while the bus ramp is in full swing.

If you have any doubts about safety at your child's school, take time to watch the bus ramp in the morning and the afternoon. Watch the teachers. Ideally, they will be spaced out for maximum coverage and visibility. They will be watching the students, traffic, and buses. When adults pick up children, they will go through what's clearly a defined process to make certain the adult and child belong together. In short, the teachers and other staff will be focused on keeping students safe.

In contrast, teachers clustered together chatting shows their focus is on the wrong things. See also: teachers and assistants on their phones while the students walk by. See also: indicators of more chaos than order in how the students are taught to move and transition on the bus ramp.

Like I mentioned, the bus ramp is the most dangerous time in the regular school day. If the school staff is lax during those vital minutes, it's fair to assume they're even more lax about safety during the less hazardous times.

What happens on the bus ramp can also tell you about how well school staff will handle emergencies. Those times reveal the level of training and accountability the principal requires of their staff.

I'll say it again. The overwhelming majority of teachers and administrators are well-trained, well-intentioned, and deeply invested in keeping our children safe. Watching the bus ramp is just how we can spot the handful who aren't.

35 Walk the Route

Data from the Consumer Product Safety Commission shows that an average of 17,000 students go to the emergency room each year from injuries sustained at school. Meanwhile, the Transportation Research Board finds that 25,000 children are injured each year *on the way to school.*

That's consistent with data from other areas. I don't think any of us are surprised to hear that our roads aren't as safe as our schools. That's not in question.

The question is: what can we do about it?

Take a Walk. As the beginning of the school year approaches, walk the route with your child. If they walk all the way to school, go the whole way. If they ride the bus, walk to the bus stop and hang out for a while. If they bike, either saddle up and ride with them or walk that route.

For best results, walk them there at the time of day they will walk to school. Do it again in the afternoon to get a sense of what will happen on their way home.

The idea is to check the route for hazards and risks, so you can train your child to manage them safely.

What to Look For. As an adult who has walked places, you already have an instinctive grasp of what's safe or dangerous with a walking route. You can build on those instincts by watching specifically for:

- Road crossings, especially those without a crosswalk or signage
- Places where the road or sidewalk are damaged
- Stretches of road without a sidewalk or bike lane
- Busy roads with fast or heavy traffic
- Blind corners where your child might not be visible
- Dangerous animals like an unleashed or unfenced dog
- Places where criminals or older children congregate
- Steep hills, either in the road or on the walking route
- Parks and paths with low visibility from the road
- Blind spots where an attacker might hide

One potential problem with this kind of exercise is that it can make children aware of risks but not of solutions for those risks. It can create more anxiety than you'd want for your child's daily experiences. That's why I recommend another aspect of this walk.

While you're looking for the risks, also look for resources that can help your child keep safe:

- Homes of friends and neighbors
- Stores and restaurants open in the appropriate hours
- Government buildings like fire stations and post offices
- Emergency call boxes in towns that have them

With a list of hazards and resources, you can sit down with your child and create a safety plan. Talk about how to be safe around the risks and take advantage of the resources. It sometimes helps to draw a map.

Do It Again. As the school year goes on, days get shorter and the route to school can become very different. It pays to walk the route at least twice more: once a week or so before Fall Back Day, and again in late November or early December as we near the Winter Solstice.

Those check-ups will let you know if the darker conditions change any safety aspects of your child's route to school. (This assumes you're in the Northern Hemisphere and a place with Daylight Savings Time).

The route home doesn't usually need a checkup, since schools let out early enough so kids get home well before sunset in most places. If they do where you live, or your child has an after-school activity that lasts until dusk, definitely do a second after-school walk-through as well.

Teens, Too. Once your kids are old enough to drive to school or ride with friends, start up your car and drive the route. Look for problem intersections, hills that might ice up in winter, and other things you know to look for that your teen doesn't.

Do this four times, twice each on the way there during the before-school hours and on the way back after school. Do each way once with you driving and once with them driving while you coach.

36 Learn to Love Location Tracking

I'm going to get Orwellian for a minute here and recommend tracking our kids' locations at all times. As a recovering libertarian and somebody who read *1984* and *Fahrenheit 451* at a particularly formative age, it bothers me a little that I feel that way.

It's worth it.

As much as I was a free-range teen and tween, and as much as I try to avoid helicopter parenting, location tracking helps ease my mind while giving my tween (now teen) more freedom and better safety.

Location tracking lets us know our kids are where they say they'll be, that they've gotten to a destination safely, and that they're on the way home. When we know that stuff, we can loosen the reins a bit because there's a safety net.

There's some irony there, claiming that we can give our kids more freedom by essentially putting them under surveillance. But ironic doesn't mean untrue. Think of it like training wheels. It lets them take more risks and explore more widely because you've set up a safety measure.

Based on my research, I have three-and-a-half favorite location tracking apps I'd like to recommend.

- **Find My Friends**, a default app for iPhone. It's good because it's simple to install and easy to use. The security is solid, and it has flexible enough functions.
- **AirDroid**, a simple and highly rated location tracking app for Android phones. I haven't used it myself, but I've heard good things from my security-conscious Android people.

- **TacticsOn** was originally built by bodyguard-to-the-stars Will Geddes for his teams to communicate while on mission. He built a civilian version of it that includes location tracking, panic buttons, and more. It costs less than $5 for lifetime, and it's what my family uses.

The "and-a-half" is for Life360. Its location tracking is part of a robust suite of functions that includes automated panic buttons and all kinds of other bells and whistles. It has a reasonable monthly fee but comes with one caveat.

In 2022, they were caught selling location data to various companies. Including location data of the children using their app. They have since stopped and apologized, but it's worth considering as you weigh your options.

Not for Everybody. To be clear, in my opinion location tracking is for every parent with a child of phone-owning age. But your child's location isn't anybody's business but yours.

Take a minute to turn off location tracking for everything but the app you chose to help you know where they are.

On an iPhone or iPad, go to Settings>Privacy>Location Services. Turn off permission for all but the one app. If they need it temporarily for any other app (like Maps) they can grant a one-time usage when the box pops up.

For an Android phone, go to Settings>Personal>Location Access. Turn off permission from there.

Once it's off, talk with your kids about why you've turned off location data so they can make fully informed decisions about that one-time tracking.

What About Buy-In? Letting you know where they are at all times might be a hard sell for some teens, especially teens who have already been using their phones without that feature active.

One of the best tools for this is a family phone contract. I cover that in detail elsewhere in this book.

37 Prepare for Weather Closures

Remember snow days? For my readers in Florida and Laos, a snow day was a beautiful thing for children in temperate climates. A cold snap hit overnight, and more snow than the local infrastructure could handle piled up on the roads. To prevent injuries to teachers and kids alike, school closed for the day.

They were pretty neat.

What wasn't as neat was when the snow happened in the middle of the day. It took a lot to close school in progress, but most people I know remember it happening at least once during their time in school, or their own children's time.

That's a hassle. The schools have to communicate with all of the parents. Buses have to be suddenly mobilized and drivers brought in from wherever they are, if the weather is safe enough for buses. Parents have to come in from work to pick up their kids. Teachers have to coordinate with administration, staff, and their own families. All while snow falls and road conditions worsen with every passing minute.

And that's just a minor, even charming, weather event. Now, imagine the same situation in a more serious emergency. Something like a tornado, sudden long-term blackout, or civil unrest.

I've said it before in this book: in the middle of an emergency is not the time to make a plan for that emergency.

The Big Questions. Your key goal in a midday snow closure or similar situation is reuniting your family as quickly and safely as possible. As you build a plan for that, consider these questions:

- How will you find out about the school closure and its circumstances?
- How will you interface with school officials to report your progress and check on your children?
- Where is everybody most likely to be?
- How many of your people have access to a car?
- How many children are old and able enough to leave school on their own?
- How many parents are close enough to the school to pick up children?
- With multiple schools, is it best to send a parent to each, or for one parent to gather everybody?
- How will everybody communicate as you gather? How will you communicate if cell phones go down?
- Where will everybody initially come together?
- If the main routes to any location are blocked, what are the best alternative routes?
- If driving is not safe or feasible, how will parents reach the children?
- What is the backup plan if somebody can't manage their part?

Another question to ask is if you need to rush to school at all. In major emergencies, the route to school can be hazardous. Is there a neighbor, grandparent, or parent of your children's friends who could fill in until you get there?

If all else fails, remember that schools are well-built, full of trained adults, and stocked with food, water, and medical supplies. During disasters, rescue and emergency workers often use them as staging areas. There are worse places for our children to wait for us as we make our way to them safely.

38 Fight Bullies with Your Brains

This chapter opened with what we can do as parents to deal with bullying in our children's schools. It helps, but it's not enough. Sooner or later every child ends up having to deal directly personally with a bully who targets them.

Dave Kovar is a leader in the martial arts industry and the developer of the Done with Bullying program. It's a realistic, compassionate, effective program you can find at martial arts schools around the country. Dave recommends:

Putting the FIST into Pacifist. Well, not really. I saw that on a shirt once and it makes me laugh every time. Dave's bully system is built on what he calls the Five-Finger-Fist. As the name implies, it consists of five steps.

Each step is an effective way to stand up when being bullied, teaching children to begin with early interventions and to use physical force only as a last resort to protect themselves or others.

You work through the steps, mentally closing each finger as you go. When the fifth step closes your thumb, your hand has become a fist and is ready for self-defense.

- **First Finger:** Listen with Empathy, giving compassionate, sincere attention to somebody who is probably hurting.
- **Second Finger:** Look for the Exit to leave if the situation doesn't immediately get better.
- **Third Finger:** Ask for Help, getting kids, teachers, bystanders, or strangers to jump in and stop violence before it starts.

- **Fourth Finger:** Hands Up, placing open hands and arms between the bully and yourself in an assertive stance, while shouting something like "Back Off!" or "Leave Me Alone!"
- **Fifth Finger:** Hands On, using whatever fighting skills your child has if the bully escalates the situation to physical violence.

Learning this system can help our children prepare for bullies and empower them to deal with the situation. As any martial artist or other trained fighters can tell you, just having that plan and confidence is often enough to get the bully to go away and bother somebody else.

When the bully doesn't, it also creates a framework for justifying self-defense with school authorities. Even in a "zero tolerance" school, it will be hard for administration to punish a child who can articulate having tried all four of the initial steps.

Practice Makes Permanent. This system works, but only if our kids practice it ahead of time. We can run through the progression, first in theory and then with role-playing. Like any other skill applied under stress, our kids must master it under controlled circumstances before they can apply it effectively "in the wild."

39 Prepare for Shootings

I don't have the words to properly express how angry, sad, and frustrated I am that school shootings remain a relevant part of modern parenting. I don't want to have to write this chapter. You don't want to need to read it.

But what we want and what we get aren't always the same thing. We need to talk about the who, where, and what of school shooting survival.

The Who. When coming up with a plan for school shootings, start with your children. Consider their ages, stages, and abilities. A kindergartner's plan for a school shooting will be different from the plan for a linebacker with a black belt during his senior year.

- **Infants and Toddlers:** These littlest ones are helpless in emergencies and rely on us and other adults completely for protection. On the bright side, they're portable and usually with us more than older children are.
- **Early Elementary:** Children this young and small cannot realistically contribute to their own safety in this situation. Our best bet is to help them learn to manage fear and to follow their teacher's directions.
- **Intermediate Grades**: Big enough and old enough to contribute to their own safety, though most likely not able to help others. Focus on how they can escape using the tools and terrain of their school.
- **Tweens and Early Teens:** With some size and maturity, they can take responsibility for their own safety. Many can also meaningfully contribute to keeping others safe as well. Most should focus on escape, but some can also learn organizing and counter-attack skills.
- **Young Adults:** Treat kids this age like you would any adult dealing with these issues. Many are ready to take leadership in a shooting situation, but we shouldn't pressure or shame those who can't.

These are generalizations, of course. Only you know what your child is capable of. The important part is to give this thought as the first step in developing a response plan.

The Where. School shootings happen at school. The more you and your child know about what it's like there, the better your plan.

This starts at the district level. Find out what the school shooting response plan is for the district and for individual schools. Learn if there is a blanket policy for all schools, or if the plan changes to fit the realities of each individual building.

Next, drill down to your child's school. Who implements the plan there? Is the plan realistic and reasonable given the staff and floor plan? Visit the school and your child's classroom and look for tactical considerations like windows, cover, and how long the hallways are.

Not every school or district is forthcoming about this information. It's not good operational security to tell just anybody exactly how you will respond to an armed attack. But as a parent, you can usually get the most important details if you're polite and insistent.

The What. What will you teach your child to do if a school shooter comes on campus?

Based on their age and abilities, plus your assessment of the district and school plan, grounds, and staff, should they follow the plan as written? If you don't see glaring issues, that's probably best.

If there are glaring issues, what can they do instead? The Run/Hide/Fight framework is popular, but I'm not a fan. It's too passive and suggests a straight line. Run until you find a place to hide, then hide there until the bad guy makes you fight.

I was taught a better alternative by Alain Burrese (who wrote the introduction to Section 4), an extremely intelligent man who trains schools and institutions about this exact thing. He prefers Escape/Deny/Attack.

- **Escape** because you're not just running, you're running toward safety, and you might be crawling, or pausing, or walking, or climbing, too.
- **Deny** because you are actively denying the shooter access to you and your location. It's not just ducking under a desk. It's barricading doors, turning off lights, filling hallways with debris, and any other thing that makes reaching you harder.
- **Attack** because "fight" feels like a boxing match or other fair encounter. Attack a shooter brutally, viciously, in numbers, and by ambush.

I can't write a perfect, one-size-fits-all plan everybody can just lift out of this book. What I've said above should help you develop the best plan possible for your family.

If you would like some help, I have created a series of courses to help families build a customized plan for each of their children. Reach out to me via email at brickcommajason@gmail.com, and we can schedule a free chat to get your family better prepared.

40   Volunteer at School

This is possibly the most valuable, and least exciting, piece of safety advice you will find in this section. Possibly the whole book.

It's exactly what it sounds like: make time to volunteer in your children's school.

The schools need you. They're understaffed and overworked, and any time you can put in frees up resources for the professionals who keep the place running.

The students need you. School staff don't have the time to give every child in class the personal attention they need. You can give a kind word, a helping hand, or just a brief moment of contact that makes a bad day better, or an already good day great.

Your kids need you. More to the point, your kids need to see evidence that you take their education seriously and are willing to go out of your way to support them.

All that, plus it can save lives.

Everybody wins.

Volunteering and Safety. A very incomplete list of the safety benefits from volunteering at our children's schools includes:

- An additional set of adult eyes to watch the kids and keep them on the straight, safe, and narrow.
- An additional set of adult eyes on the adults to watch for predators in the worst place to find them.
- We are on scene to help in emergencies big and small.
- We get to know the staff and other volunteers, so we have a good sense of the adults responsible for our children's safety.
- We get to know the kids, so we have a more informed sense of any trouble our children tell us about.
- Staff get to know us, and by knowing us become more invested in doing right by our children.
- We become familiar with the school grounds, so we can craft better safety plans.
- We become familiar with the school safety procedures, both policy-wise and in daily practice.
- We contribute to a safer community by providing help and role-modeling to a wider circle of children.
- We visibly give our time, attention, and effort to our kids' education. Even if they never mention it, they see that we did.

There's also a deterrent factor. A school with more adults on-site is a safer and more secure school. In the rare cases that a stranger opts to target a school, they are likely to target one with fewer adults on-site.

Volunteering Opportunities. With my two sons, I've volunteered as a classroom assistant, chess coach, karate teacher, wrestling coach, field trip chaperone, and drama club dad. Before I even became a parent, in my capacity as a martial arts school owner, I volunteered as a classroom teacher, PE teacher, reading coach, chess coach (again), and presenter to whole schools on various safety topics.

There are so many ways to help out at schools. Some put us with our kids, in the same room. Others, often better as they age into those years when our very existence embarrasses them, keep us separate but still on-site. All of them support our kids, support our schools, and keep them safer.

Volunteering usually starts by contacting somebody at your child's school: a teacher, principal, coach, or PTA leader. They'll identify where the need is greatest. From there, the next step will be getting some kind of certification or background check at the district level. After that, you coordinate with somebody at your school about how and when you will volunteer.

Finding the Time. For those of us fortunate enough to work from home, or parents without a job outside the house, this is easy enough. We just prioritize this and make room for it in our schedules. It's just as simple, but admittedly harder, for parents who work swing and night shifts.

It's not so easy for parents who work during the day. Start by checking the volunteering policy at your company. Many large corporations have volunteer leave options, where you can take a certain amount of paid time off in a year to volunteer for schools and nonprofits. It won't be enough to go in every week, but it will be better than nothing.

If your employer doesn't have volunteer leave, you have two options. One is to get some flex time, letting you come in late or leave early on a day you want to volunteer. The other is to talk your employer into starting a volunteer leave policy, or convince them that having you in schools a few times a month is good publicity and part of your job.

It won't be easy, but if you can make it happen, it will be worth it.

School Safety Action Plan

General advice doesn't do much good, especially for people with free time as limited as active parents. Here's a quick checklist of the most vital action items you can start with today about safety at school.

Do these this week and you're on your way to a safer family:

- ❏ Confirm your phone is set to receive safety notifications from your child's school and school district.
- ❏ Take ten minutes to observe the teachers at your school bus ramp.
- ❏ Set up location tracking with your child's phone.

Find an hour soon and take action to become even safer:

- ❏ Identify the person most directly responsible for your child's safety at school, and get their email, phone number, and social media information.
- ❏ Drive or walk your child's route to school, with an eye toward potential hazards and places to get help.
- ❏ Have a strategy session with your child about what to do in a school shooting or similar emergency.

Make time for these important long-term projects to become the safest family on your block:

- ❏ Figure out your principal's schedule well enough to engineer a five-minute casual chat.
- ❏ Develop a complete family plan for emergencies that close school in the middle of the day.
- ❏ Sign up to volunteer at your child's school for a few hours each month.

SECTION 5

ONLINE SAFETY

Introduction by Maria Kristina-Hayden

Maria-Kristina Hayden is an Intelligence Officer turned Wall Street cyber wargamer turned public speaker, founder, and CEO. Her latest venture OUTFOXM™ is a cyber hygiene and wargaming company dedicated to improving global levels of cyber safety. Find tips and resources at www.outfoxm.com and on social media at @ outfoxm.

The stinging sensation in his lungs snapped him out of his trance. He realized he had completely stopped breathing. AmsterdamBabe09 threatened to send the picture he sent last night…the one without his pants on…to his entire school and travel soccer team. Coaches, counselors, friends, bullies, everyone.

Phone nearly slipping from his sweaty hand as he stood up, he paced. Locked his bedroom door, kicked a shoe out of the way and paced. Visions of his friends and mentors seeing that picture flashed before his eyes. Dread, fear, and shame welled up as he muttered, "Can't tell Dad—he'll kill me. Can't tell Mom. She'll tell Dad."

Falling back into his chair, he leaned back and searched the ceiling for answers.

Unfortunately, this sextortion scenario is happening to someone, somewhere, now as you read this. From here the situation can take a variety of turns, depending on whether the fear and shame give way to despair, anger, or something else.

The good news is, it's preventable. And figure-outable if it does happen. Believe it or not, so are the rest of the largest online risks to children and families. This chapter is your roadmap for understanding which risks to focus on, how to reduce them, and how to detect warning signs if tricky situations have already begun.

41 Post Where You Were

Unlike most safety books, I don't spend much time here on preventing financial crime. Identity theft sucks, but it's not a direct threat to family safety. The same goes for burglaries, stolen cars, and purse snatching. Also, there are plenty of really great resources about stopping property crime.

In this chapter, though, I will talk about how social media posts link to crime. Most of the time those are property crimes, but poor timing and some bad luck can escalate them into home invasions, assaults, and even murder.

How It Started. On a visit to the grandparents' house in the next town over, you take a series of photos. They show grandpa reading a book, grandma showing them how to garden, and the spread at the picnic table in the backyard. Everybody is smiling. The sun is just right.

In a quiet moment, you post a spread of your favorites with a heartfelt and beautiful message about how much you love getting all three generations together.

All of your friends like it. Many comment to say hi to your parents, who many of them have met over the years.

For another take, your college-age daughter goes out with her friends on a Saturday night. It's a festival of mild debauchery starting with dinner and moving through a half-dozen clubs and bars on the strip near campus. They wrap things up at a friend's apartment for a few more drinks, then crash on whichever couches are nearest.

She documents the entire thing, posting selfies from her dorm room getting ready, of the squad gathering in the lobby, at dinner, on the street, at each club, and on the way home.

Her friends across the world celebrate the night with her, commenting live. A video of a drunken headstand even goes viral.

How It's Going. Both of the situations seem innocuous, even common. But, from a safety standpoint, they're not safe.

The photos from the family gathering tell anybody looking that you're not home. Modern burglars case houses on social media, looking for photos of where the owners keep their valuables. If they see that you're gone for the night, it's an open invitation.

Again, that's property crime. But what if you come home in the middle of it? Or if you're at grandma's but your fourteen-year-old son stayed home alone?

I won't go into detail about the risks involved with a young woman posting her location and level of inebriation publicly in real time. Now that we're thinking about it in this particular way, I'm sure your imagination can manage that on its own.

The point is this: criminals have access to your feed. Some can use the information there to hurt your family. We shouldn't give them that information.

How to Do It. There's a simple rule that keeps us safe while still letting us celebrate and share our best moments across social media.

Post where you've been, not where you are.

The best way to apply this is to wait until an event is over. Whether it's a night out, a weekend with the grandparents, or a two-week vacation, store your pictures and post them once you've returned home. That time lag resolves most of the security issues associated with this risk.

Not everybody is happy to do that. Posting more frequently is part of how they enjoy their time in the world. If that's you, try posting at the end of each day. On a multi-day trip, assemble the best images and make a single post about how great that particular day was.

At the very least, avoid posting in real time. On a pub crawl, for example, post about the second bar while you're in the third. This still broadcasts that you're not at home, but at least it won't tell stalkers and assorted creepers where you are right now.

42 No Bedrooms, No Bathrooms

This one is easy to understand, but harder to make happen.

In researching online safety, I came across a piece of advice that every expert I spoke with agreed on. With our kids, set a strict no bedroom/no bathroom policy for any device that connects to the internet.

Wait, but Why? The no bedrooms, no bathrooms rule helps with your child's safety in three important ways.

First, it removes privacy from their online experience. They have less temptation and opportunity to take, post, or view risqué images and videos. They're more visible while they're online, so we can watch their body language. We get a glimpse of what apps and networks they use, so we can research how they work and where they're easily spoofed or exploited.

Second, it fights some of the sleep issues that many teens (and adults) experience with screen time. You probably already know that screen time in bed means getting to sleep later and having lower-quality sleep when it comes. Keeping devices in the common areas means that's no longer a factor. Kids go to bed with no screens within reach.

Third, it makes evenings and weekends more family oriented. Even a living room full of people all looking at their screens separately is more unified than a house where everybody is having screen time while shut in their own rooms.

Yeah, Okay, But... This advice makes sense, and it's universally supported by the relevant experts I trust. It also gets the most pushback of all the advice I ever give.

That's because the kids are going to fight against this tooth and nail. At least a lot of parents assume so.

The easy way around this is to make it a rule from the first use of screen time for our kids. If they grow up with public areas only for screens, they won't view it as anything unusual. Eventually, you'll get some chatter about how their friends don't have the rule, but there shouldn't be too much trouble.

Of course, that depends on setting that rule early. If you've already missed that window, putting the rule in place can feel like a punishment. It can seem unfair, even to you.

In that case, the conversation will go easier the earlier you have it. Sit down and discuss the new rule. Talk about the reasons it's important. Let things wander into a general Q&A session about online safety and what your kids view as the biggest threats. Lean in to how being online in spaces you share with them helps you be a protector and resource. Use every trick in the book.

I'm not promising this will be easy. I'm just saying it will be worth it.

A Half Measure. Although what I'm about to suggest is not as safe as a strict no bedroom/no bathroom policy, it can accomplish many of its goals while still feeling less draconian.

Start with the no bedroom/no bathroom policy and create benchmarks to earn that privilege and trust. Tie it to age, grades, or other metrics and allow set windows for private screen time. Allow successful teens to work their way up to full authority over their device usage and set up rules to scale back those privileges if problems develop.

They Are Watching. If you didn't like what you just read, you're *really* going to hate reading this.

One of the best ways to get buy-in from our kids with this is to observe the rule ourselves. We can also benefit from less before-bed doomscrolling and binging Netflix with our family instead of apart from them.

This can be especially important and helpful if we're trying to establish the rule after tweens are already used to private space phone privileges.

I don't know what to tell you about how you can pass the time when going to the bathroom. Maybe keep some magazines on hand?

43 Watch In-Game Chat

Here's the thing about online predators: they're smart. Maybe not smart, but good at what they do. The ones who aren't good get caught quickly.

They know we're watching social media and checking text messages and messaging apps. They're aware we can look in on their emails. To the degree that online forums are still a thing kids use, the predators know that we know how to use them.

Because of that, the predators have found a new corner of the internet to lurk in.

In-Game Chat. This probably isn't something you don't know, but many games have online multiplayer options where people can play in real time against people all over the world. A lot of those include some kind of in-game chat feature.

These run all the way from a simple chat box in one corner of the screen, to full video and audio like you get with Zoom meetings at work.

Online predators have for years used these to approach potential victims.

This makes sense. Predators of all kinds go to where the prey is, and these chats are virtual playgrounds with less supervision than public parks. Because games are targeted at different age groups, it sorts the population for the age each predator prefers. Playing a game with a child creates an automatic connection, a way to begin establishing conversation.

These chats are less well-known to many parents as being risky, and many game companies don't have the security budget to monitor what goes on there.

What Can We Do About It? As always, the most important thing we can do about this is to have a warm and supportive relationship with our kids. That way, if something weird is happening online, they feel safe and comfortable coming to us.

In addition to that, it pays to research the games our kids play regularly. Find out if they have online multiplayer mode, and if that mode has any kind of chat. Learn how the chat works and what security measures are in place.

If you're savvy with computer research, you can look for reports on any specific game's chat security. By the time a game is a few months old, the right people know how safe or dangerous its chat environment is. Whether that "right person" is you or somebody you trust, it's worth it to find out.

Another good defense is playing the games with our kids from time to time. We get to know the game and its chat function while we keep an eye out for the sorts of people who make contact. As a bonus, we get some quality time with our kids, enjoying something they're passionate about.

Christian Gaming. Since starting my show, I've been approached by a handful of Christian game companies offering an online game that shares the wholesome values of their faith. I'm convinced these people mean well, and I've even had one on the program.

Depending on which study you read, the Christian community has either the same number of sexual predators, or a larger number, compared to the population at large.

This isn't to bash on Christianity, or any other faith. But it is to warn you that Christian games, even those that advertise a safer environment because of who's online, need just as much watching as any other option.

44 Take Cyberbullying Seriously

Cyberbullying is in some ways like human trafficking and the fentanyl crisis. It's a scary buzzword that lots of poorly informed media personalities like to throw around, but it's often poorly defined and misused in context.

What is cyberbullying, really? How bad is it? Most important, what can we do about it when it enters our children's lives?

What Is Cyberbullying? Ask a hundred different people to define cyberbullying and you'll get a hundred different answers. My favorite comes from UNICEF.

UNICEF defines cyberbullying as repeated behavior, using digital technologies, to scare, anger, or shame those who are targeted.

UNICEF goes on to give some concrete examples:

- Spreading lies about or posting embarrassing photos or videos of someone on social media

- Sending hurtful, abusive, or threatening messages, images, or videos via messaging platforms
- Impersonating someone and sending mean messages to others on their behalf or through fake accounts

Cyberbullying is bullying. It's cowards trying to feel better about themselves by hurting, scaring, and humiliating people they think are weaker. The only difference between this and the old way is they use the digital world to make it happen.

How Bad Can It Get? Cyberbullying carries with it all of the damage and risks of classic bullying. Research by organizations like UNICEF and the CDC have linked it to:

- Reduced self-esteem
- Dropping grades
- Depression
- Anxiety
- Eating disorders
- Increased vulnerability to predators
- Sleep disorders
- Headaches
- Digestive issues
- Lowered immune systems
- Self-harm
- Suicidal ideation

One argument some make to suggest that cyberbullying isn't severe is that nobody can beat someone up over the internet. Although it's true they can't directly do physical damage, a 2022 study published in the *Journal of the American Medical Association* found that teens who suffered from cyberbullying were four times as likely to have suicidal thoughts and fantasies than those who were not.

Although the exact numbers vary, that's just one of many studies that have found a link between cyberbullying and increased instances of self-harm. Cyberbullying can and does physically hurt victims.

There's also one way cyberbullying is much worse than the in-person version. With in-person bullying, there was always an end. Even the worst day at school would be over, and at home kids could spend time safe with people who weren't mean to them.

Social media, texts, and chat rooms are there 24/7. If our kids stay online all day, they are vulnerable to cyberbullying all day.

What Can We Do About It? Defense against cyberbullying starts with something that helps protect our kids from many other attacks: build trust from early on with your children. If they know we love them and will help them with problems, they also know they can come to us if they are being bullied online.

Beyond that long-term project, we can also do a number of simpler things to help them avoid or handle cyberbullying:

- Keep all screens in common areas of the home so we can see our children as they interact online.
- Talk regularly and specifically about online issues.
- Stay educated about online apps, sites, and trends.
- Tell our kids to never respond to any cyberbullying, just record the message and move on.
- Never blame our children or tell them it's "no big deal."
- Encourage our kids to put the phone down if cyberbullying starts. Bullies often go away if they don't get any response.
- Insist our children promise to never engage in cyberbullying themselves.
- Do not make confiscating devices part of your family discipline structure. It only makes kids less likely to come to us about online issues.

We don't want our kids to respond to cyberbullies, but that doesn't mean there shouldn't be a response. It should come from us.

As tempting as it might be to log in and start a flame war with the jerk who tried to hurt our kid, that's not the kind of response I have in mind. Instead, we build a case.

Start by printing or screenshotting the bullying messages. Track the time, date, and usernames. Once you have a healthy record, bring it to school administrators or counselors. Just like with physical bullying, make it clear that you won't let this slide. You won't go away until the cyberbullying goes away.

If the schools won't or can't do anything, or if the cyberbullying escalates to threats, take the same information to the police. Harassment is illegal, and cyberbullying is harassment.

45 Know the Signs of Online Grooming

Some concerns parents come to me with are very bad, but also very unlikely. School shootings are on that list. Other concerns are very common, but really no big deal for prepared families. Basic first-aid situations are on that list.

Then there are situations that are both very bad and relatively common. Online sexual predation is one of those.

FBI statistics from last year estimate half a million online predators are active on any given day and that a quarter of children report some sort of sexual exploitation attempt by their eighteenth birthday. Of those attempts, nearly 90 percent happen in chatrooms or via text messaging.

It might even be worse than that. Fully 40 percent of young people said they never reported the "worst thing that had happened to them online" to any adult.

To protect our kids from this, our best line of defense is to know what online grooming looks like so we can stop it in its tracks. Because we can't watch the actual predators, and we shouldn't monitor every moment our kids spend online, we need to focus on two areas.

Red Flags While Kids Are Online. In most cases, we are the first line of defense for our children. Online, though, our children will be the first to see inappropriate behavior. If we train them about what sorts of behaviors to watch out for, they can tell us and we can investigate.

The most common warning signs to teach our children to watch for include:

- Adults and older teens in child games and chat areas
- Anybody using a fake profile
- Asking for personal information
- Steering the conversation toward sex or relationships
- Asking kids to keep secrets
- Sharing photos or videos of any type
- Moving from public chats to private chats

We can teach our children to tell us whenever they encounter this sort of behavior. Not every one is a sure sign of an online predator (for example, many otherwise well-intentioned teens set up dummy accounts to escape parental overwatch), but we should investigate it every time.

Offline Red Flags. From the outside, grooming can look like normal phone or computer use. Add to that the sad fact that groomers can be good at convincing children not to talk about their online activities, and it can be a challenge to catch in the earliest stages.

That said, a few changes in our kids' behavior can be early indicators that not all is well with their online friends:

- Increased amounts of time spent online
- Becoming secretive about what they do online
- Switching tabs or screens when people approach
- Changes in language, especially about sex
- Sudden emotional changes
- New possessions you're not sure how they got
- Disproportionate messages from online acquaintances they don't know in person
- Skipping activities they used to enjoy
- Receiving phone calls from numbers you don't recognize

As with others' behavior online, not every one of these is a certain indicator that a predator has approached our children. What tween or teen doesn't have sudden emotional changes at one time or another?

What you're looking for is a pattern of changes from their previous behavior. If it's enough for you to notice, it's enough for you to look into.

Important Reminder. When most of us imagine an online predator, we think of an overweight guy with a patchy beard that our children have never seen before.

Although this happens, the overwhelming majority of online and offline sexual abuse comes from people the children and their parents know.

Make sure your children watch for suspicious behavior just as carefully from teachers, coaches, friends' older brothers, and all the other adults in their lives. It's terrible that this is something they have to do, but sometimes terrible things are true.

46 **Practice Good Information Hygiene**

It's no myth that bad guys are on the internet, looking for ways to break into systems and steal our vital information. An incomplete list of major companies that have suffered data breaches in the past few years includes Yahoo, LinkedIn, CapitalOne, Uber, Home Depot, Facebook, Marriott, Adobe, Twitter, Experian, Equifax, and eBay. These are not exactly fly-by-night operations lacking a strong security budget.

This kind of breach is serious, but it's not what should scare us as parents. I say this for two reasons.

First, these breaches are about identity theft and financial crime. They're important, but they're not a hazard to our kids' health and safety. I'd rather lose a thousand dollars than see my kids hurt any day of the week, and so would you.

Second, there's very little we can do about information security at that level. Those breaches had nothing to do with the customers' password strength or online behavior. They came from issues at the enterprise level. You and I could study the problem full-time and lock down our home networks, but none of that would impact how IBM keeps their data.

What We Can Change. Part of safe parenting is putting our efforts—and our worries—where they can do our family actual good. We should watch the news for major breaches that impact us but focus on our personal information security. I have some bad news about that.

We give a surprising amount of information to the bad guys, voluntarily, for free, every day. For example:

- That sign supporting the cheerleading team tells anybody driving past the house that a teenage girl lives there.
- A "Proud Wife of a Deployed Soldier" T-shirt or bumper sticker tells everybody the husband is gone for months at a time.
- The sports decal on the back of a minivan tells local predators a child's name and a vital interest they can engage them about.
- A team jersey gives away the child's name and lets people find out where they'll be on certain evenings.

Those are real-life instances of data leakage that we make all the time without realizing it. In each case, we give bad guys information they could use to make hurting our families easier. Always remember: the most important factor when a criminal chooses a victim is likelihood of success. When we give information like this away, it improves that likelihood and makes us more attractive targets.

It gets even worse when you look online.

- That Christmas morning Instagram post tells bad guys how much loot is at your home or when and where you'll be on vacation.
- Your daughter's TikTok video has posters and photos in her bedroom that give away her hobbies and what school she attends.
- The foodie photo you posted on date night lets anybody interested know you're not home right now.
- A pair of anniversary vacation photos lets people know you're away, and the teenagers you're always bragging about might be home alone.

Do me a favor. Stop reading this and go scroll through your primary social media feedback about two weeks. Look at it from the point of view of somebody who wants to hurt your family. How much information could they get in just a few minutes? Seriously, go do that now. I'll wait.

In the military and spycraft world, they call this OPSEC: OPerational SECurity. Parenting safely includes watching how much information we give potential bad guys and keeping our business more...well, *our* business.

This isn't such an urgent matter for our two-to-five year olds, since they rarely spend time unsupervised and don't yet have social media accounts. Developing this habit early, though, can help them keep it when they're older. It can also help us train our tweens and teens to stay safe online and in real life, when they go out and about on their own.

47 Learn to Love YouTube

Want to know a secret?

Back when I was getting my black belt, I worked a day job in the tech sector. That's not the secret. I'm pretty open about that part of my life. I was young and needed the money. It is, though, why I know the secret. Here it is.

Half the IT people you know, and all of the coders, look stuff up online every day to help them do their jobs. They haven't memorized every spec of every piece of hardware and software ever made. They don't know every scrap of code in every language their boss requires. They know how and where to find the information they need, and how to understand what they find even when it's written by experts.

There's no reason not to do the same thing with our online safety. For every app your teen wants to download, there are three tutorials and a safety analysis on YouTube. For every technical issue you have securing your home network, there are a dozen tech firms who've posted easy tutorials. Everything you're worried about as a full-time parent but amateur online safety expert, there's a professional giving good advice.

Sometimes all you need is an entry-level introduction or the professional opinion of somebody in the field. Other times you need to start there, then follow the rabbit hole until you've become well-informed about that topic yourself.

It's not cheating. Professionals do it all the time, and so can we.

This is especially helpful for parents, because we're a step behind on tech stuff. For most of us, we use the internet like somebody asking for directions in a language they studied in college. Our kids are native speakers. Looking up videos can help us get closer to parity.

Even better, they give us topics and vocabulary to talk meaningfully with our kids about what they do online. Those meaningful talks become constant, clear, caring communication as you work together to get them the virtual freedom they want while also keeping them safe.

The web is filled with great safety resources, but here are my top-ten YouTube channels for family safety.

- Binary Tattoo
- Get Licensed—Frontline Security
- Managing Violence Podcast
- Fire Department Chronicles
- Parenting for Connection with Robbin Mccanne
- Relationship Rx with Laura Dabney
- City Prepping
- Active Self Protection
- *Wired Magazine's* Tradecraft Series
- Safety Kay

Honorable mention: *Safest Family on the Block*. It has over one hundred interviews with world-class safety experts in everything from martial arts, to fire safety, to child psychology, to nutrition. It's not on the list only because it's mine, but I'm proud of it and I'm still amazed by the quality of people who've come on the show. Please do check it out.

48 Bring in a Buddy to Deter Risque Posting

This simple parenting hack comes to us from Cat Coode of Binary Tattoo, one of the smartest people working in internet safety and data privacy today. It was just one of the many things I learned when I interviewed her for my show.

I do not have daughters, but Cat does, and as far as I can tell this checks out. Cat reports it has worked for many people she's given the advice to.

The Problem. As teen (and even tween) girls become women, they face the temptation to post photos of themselves either wearing revealing outfits, or emphasizing parts of their bodies commonly associated with pin-up posters. Although it's disconcerting to a lot of parents, it's a natural part of the modern teen experience. Teens are discovering sex and sexuality, and some of them want to show some of that off...especially if they have a particular potential viewer in mind.

This is natural and normal, and the last thing we want to do is oversexualize or slut shame the teenage girls we're responsible for. On the other hand, the internet is very public and the internet is forever. The people she has in mind might not be the only ones viewing it, and some of those people could become fixated or target her as a victim.

It's true that teen boys face many of the same temptations and pressures. However, the risks aren't as great. Social shame for being sexual just isn't as bad for boys, and the likelihood of attracting a stalker or predator is lower. That seems sexist, and it is...but only because the realities of safety are sexist.

Bottom line: a sixteen-year-old girl posting a bikini photo on her Instagram isn't bad or wrong, and it certainly isn't immoral, but it can be risky. So what do we do about that?

The Solution. Almost all of us have that one friend. The friend is male. He's middle-aged. He's a little overweight. He's not actually a creep, but he sometimes comes off as a little creepy.

The next time that friend comes over to visit, have him mention in passing the photo you're concerned about. Not in a "hey, your parents told me about this and here's my advice" way. Oh, no. That won't do the trick. Have him mention it in a "I saw your red bikini photo on your Instagram. It's really nice" way.

According to Cat, this never fails to at the very least get daughters to tighten up their privacy controls. Some of them stop posting the revealing photos entirely.

It's not the nicest thing you'll ever have done, but I'm told it's very effective.

The Better Solution. Of course, that's what to do if your daughter is posting in an unsafe way despite your advice and warnings. The better solution comes in two parts:

- **Part One:** Have her already informed and intelligent about the internet, its risks, and the specifics of privacy controls and curating her online contacts list. If she's on top of this, a few racy photos won't be a problem because they're not going out where bad guys can see them.

- **Part Two**: Have an open, honest, and mutually respectful dialogue about sex from an early age. With that in place, your daughter's behavior around revealing photos, dating, sex, and potential online predators will be, as the kids say, "on point."

Both of those solutions happen through a long history of communication, listening, and teaching over the course of your daughter's childhood. It's worth the effort, starting today. But if that's not in place yet, the above plan works really well.

49   Lock Down Your Home Network

When most of us were growing up, we only had to worry about bad guys coming into our homes through the doors and windows. Sure, there was that one movie where somebody snuck in through a crawlspace, but even the corner cases were still physical intrusions.

Today, criminals can access our houses and children without setting foot in our homes. If we're lucky, all they do is steal data and our identities. If we're not, they use it to gather information before a physical invasion.

That means it's on us as parents to secure our home networks as well as we secure our doors and windows.

Doing that can be intimidating. We understand about window pins and deadbolts, but computer security is a newer skill for humans in general. The good news here is that we can manage a few simple things that will lock down our home networks to keep bad guys out and our information in.

Change Your Default Home Network. Technical types call your network's name the "SSID," which stands for service set identifier. When you go to log in to Wi-Fi, the list of network names it shows is the list of SSIDs in the area. Each router comes with a default name set by the manufacturer.

If you keep that name, anybody searching for nearby Wi-Fi knows the name. If cybercriminals know that name, they also know the manufacturer for your modem. This information can tell them the vulnerabilities and what they need to beat your home network security.

Google "change my network name and password for [router model]" and you will find instructions for how to change your router's name to something without this vulnerability.

While you're at it, update the password to something secure. Change the password every six months.

Create Secondary Networks. If you use only one network for your home, guests, and all connected devices, you've put all your security eggs into a single basket. A one-time guest who casually asks for your Wi-Fi password then has permanent access to every connected device in your home.

To avoid this, the experts I've spoken with recommend using three different home networks:

- One for the family, defined in this case as the people who actually live in your home
- One for friends, defined in this case as anybody you allow to use Wi-Fi in your home who doesn't live there
- One for connected devices like smart thermostats, security cameras, and other parts of the Internet of Things

Your family network will be the most secure, with the fewest people and devices accessing it. That makes it safer to keep sensitive information on there. The other two are less secure, so you partition them off with separate networks.

You can buy three different routers, one for each network, and set them up with your provider. This is the most secure option, but also the most complex and expensive. Most homes are fine with a VLAN, or virtual local area network. A quick internet search will find you plenty of tutorials on how to make that happen.

Keep Your Equipment Healthy. The longer any particular piece of hardware, firmware, or software has existed, the more time cybercriminals have had to find its vulnerabilities. Sometimes the triggers for updates include information about an attempted or successful virus or exploit, which the manufacturer is trying to fix.

Beyond that, older gear of any kind wears out, gets overloaded with processes, or physically breaks. When it breaks, your performance isn't the only thing that suffers. Your security is often made less effective.

That's why it's important to keep your software and firmware up to date by accepting updates from the manufacturer whenever they come across. Some updates aren't automatic, so check with your vendor's tech support website every six months.

Turn Off Convenient Vulnerabilities. Lots of security is a trade-off between safety and convenience. Keeping your best jewelry in a safe means it's harder to access on date night, but also less likely to get stolen if somebody breaks in.

Two specific virtual conveniences create disproportionate security risks, so experts recommend you turn them off.

- **Universal plug and play**, which makes it easier for your devices to discover and connect with your home network. You need it on whenever you install a new device, but at all other times leave it inactive. That way nobody can connect devices to your network without your knowledge and permission.
- **Remote access**, a function that does exactly what it sounds like. Unless you need admin-level functionality while you're away from home, it's smart to make sure nobody else can get that.

You can disable both through your router's web interface. If you're not sure how to get there, do a Google search including your router's manufacturer and model.

50 Create a Family Phone Contract

Cell phones are a lot like cars. A tween or teen with a cell phone has freedom, a tool that makes them feel closer to adulthood, and greater access to friends and events. They feel the power that comes with extra independence and control.

Also like cars, that phone comes with risks. Their access to information, including harmful and false information, no longer filters through the lens of your experience. The access predators have to them increases exponentially, as does the potential danger from screen addiction and cyberbullying

A family phone contract can expand on those benefits and reduce the risks.

What Is a Family Phone Contract? It's a written, signed agreement between you and your child about how members of the family will use their phones.

You can find versions of them online, but most of them are terrible. They're overly simplistic. They try to be one-size-fits-all, meaning none of them perfectly fit any given situation.

Worse, they are one-sided. Contracts work best when both signers have skin in the game. If it's just a piece of paper you make them sign that restricts them but doesn't impact you, you will have less buy-in and compliance.

A good family phone contract consists of five parts:

1. A listing of the people and devices it covers

2. The promises parents make to the child about phone use in the family

3. The promises the child makes the parents about phone use in the family

4. What happens when somebody breaks a promise

5. A process for changing the agreement

I have a whole online course on this. I'd love for you to check it out, but I'll give you the basics for each part right here.

Listing of People and Devices. This has two considerations: your family constellation and your device situation.

The contract is for one kid and their phone. How many adults need to be involved? A married couple or a single parent has a simple constellation, but blended families and parents living apart (with or without step-parents) requires different handling. Neither is better or worse than the other. They're just different animals.

For devices, decide what the contract covers. It can be just the phone, or expanded to include all mobile devices your child uses, or you can broaden it further to include the home network and devices at school.

Your Promises. I like to start with the commitments parents make because it means you're leading by example.

In this section, list your commitments about your child's phone. Things like how you will respect their privacy, how much you will pay for upgrades or replacements, and how quickly you will respond to texts and calls.

If you want, you can also include restrictions on how you use your phone. For example, my son's contract includes my promise to not text and drive and to put my phone away during dinner.

Their Promises. Here's what most people think of when they hear about family phone contracts: the restrictions you put on your child in exchange for having their own phone.

Every child's needs are different, but a few things to consider:

- A phone curfew
- Password discipline
- Keeping location tracking on
- How quickly they will respond to parental texts
- Guidelines on how much or where they will use their phones
- Promising to ask for help if they end up in a bad situation
- Not cyberbullying
- Rules about sharing personal information
- Rules about online purchases
- Rules for installing new apps

There's also the matter of sexting and pornography. Every family has their own approach to both, but bear in mind that it's unrealistic to set a "Don't, Ever" policy with this. Instead, use the opportunity to have an informed and open conversation about sex and phones, laying the groundwork for later decisions your teen will make.

Breach of Contract. A section of the contract that details the consequences of breaking promises serves two functions.

It means nobody is surprised by the consequences. Your child can't say a measure is too harsh because they knew from the beginning what to expect. You're not put in a position of having to come up with something on the spot.

It also changes the conversation when your child messes up. The default tone is you (the authority) against them (the person who made a mistake). This makes the contract the bad guy. You both agreed to the consequence for an infraction, and it's up to you *as a team* to implement it and handle the situation with maturity and grace.

Consider including the consequences for your own breach of contract in this section. Fair is fair.

Amendments. A contract perfect for a thirteen year old getting their first phone is inappropriate for that same child as a high school senior with an after-school job. The amendments section details how to change the contract, ideally in three different situations.

First, it handles what I just described. A quarterly, semiannual, or annual review to make changes as your child ages is just good sense. Detail when it will happen, and what it takes to make a change.

Second, put in a process for temporary reprieves. It's fair to cancel a phone curfew for an overnight visit with friends, for example. Set up exactly how that happens and include some protection against asking one parent after another says no.

Third, include language about making quick changes to ideas you liked but didn't work out in reality.

As a Team. In my experience, there are three ways to approach putting a family phone contract into action:

- Create the contract and make your child sign it if they want a phone.
- Create the contract, then negotiate changes with your child until you have an agreeable final contract.
- Build the contract together as a team, taking your needs and your kid's wants into account.

The third option is the best, if you have time and your child is old enough to participate meaningfully. The second option works well for busier families and younger children.

Don't use the first option.

Online Safety Action Plan

General advice doesn't do much good, especially for people with free time as limited as active parents. Here's a quick checklist of the most vital action items you can start with today about safety online.

Do these this week and you're on your way to a safer family:

- ❏ Change the password for your home router.
- ❏ Turn off universal plug & play, and remote access, for your home network.
- ❏ Create a folder in your home's main computer where you store screenshots of cyberbullying, potential online grooming, and similar problematic interactions.

Find an hour soon and take action to become even safer:

- ❏ Set and enforce the "no bedrooms, no bathrooms" policy.
- ❏ For one week, watch a YouTube video about online safety while waiting in the car for your kids to finish school, practice, or some similar event.
- ❏ Play your kids' favorite online game with them, paying special attention to in-game chat options.

Make time for these important long-term projects to become the safest family on your block:

- ❏ Develop the habit of posting only where you were on social media.
- ❏ Take time to learn about in-game chat for the games your kids play most often.
- ❏ Write, go over, and sign a family device contract for each person in your family.

SECTION 6

SAFER SEX AND RELATIONSHIPS

Introduction by Liza Draper

Liza Draper spent five years delivering federally funded, evidence-based comprehensive sexual education for the NH Department of Health and Human Services, focusing on pregnancy and STI prevention, along with adolescent development, affirmative consent, gender identity, and healthy relationships. She has provided in-depth training on sexual health and inclusivity not only to students but also to parents, educators, faith groups, and medical professionals.

Far too many adults steer away from honest conversations with kids about real world threats to their health and happiness. This chapter touches on consent, age-appropriate sex ed, stalking, sexting, and more.

Why? Because today's kids face challenges a lot sooner than we think—and information is their best protection. Risk-taking in these areas can have serious, lifelong consequences. If we want our children to find loving life partners, we need to talk with them about sex.

Being accepting, affirming, and accurate about this taboo subject with your children isn't easy. Were your parents comfortable explaining reproduction? Right. Few of us have models of adults openly discussing this subject.

It's natural to feel as though you are entering a minefield. That's what makes Jason's down-to-earth, pragmatic approach even more valuable. He offers sound strategies to help you overcome paralyzing awkwardness. You can use the techniques Jason teaches so your kids recognize the signs of unhealthy relationships, know how to avoid unplanned pregnancy—and understand the dangers of sharing digital images.

I urge you to read this chapter more than once. Chances are your children are already trying to cope on their own with some of the situations Jason describes. They shouldn't have to—it's your job to provide the information they need. Feeling too anxious to take advantage of Jason's suggestions? Think again about what having a safe family is worth. Then do some deep breathing. Then start the conversation.

You've got this.

51 Talk About Sex Early and Often

Abusers and predators target children at every age level. The best defense against those criminals is to talk openly about sex and sexuality from early stages.

Of course, different ages require different approaches. Explaining basic anatomy to a toddler is different from advising a college student about sex, and both are different from how to talk with a full-grown adult about whether their partner is abusive. I reviewed the advice and literature from a veritable tribe of experts on the topic, and here's what they advised for each age group.

Birth to Age 2. Even though a baby can't answer, they can hear you talk and observe how you behave around their bodies. Begin by using the anatomically correct terms for their genitals. Be matter of fact, using "penis," "vagina," and "anus" the same way you would say "knee," "nose," or "finger."

This normalizes, from the beginning, talking about sexual organs. It also gives you a default name for those various body parts. If your child shows up later using a different term, it alerts you to find out who taught them that and under what circumstances.

Ages 2 to 5. At these ages, you can begin discussing consent. Start with lessons about setting and asserting boundaries to set the stage for fully understanding consent. Respecting "no" from our children, especially about their bodies, teaches them to respect that in others and demand that respect in return.

This is also an appropriate age to start talking about how babies happen, beginning with their own birth story and the birth stories of babies entering your family and extended network.

Finally, any experienced parent knows that this is the age where children start touching themselves. Take the opportunity to discuss what's for public time, and what's for exploring and discovering alone. Make sure they know that you're always available for questions about these things, even though they aren't for everybody.

Ages 6 to 8. This is when kids start applying what you've taught them out in the world. It's the time to reinforce lessons about bodies, parts, consent, and respect when you find teachable moments, and discuss or role-play how they might respond if it comes up during their lives outside the home. Beyond that, this is when to expand the discussion to two additional fields.

Start discussing sexual safety in the digital realm. This includes online chat with strangers, sexting and sextortion, and warning signs that somebody they meet on the internet might be a predator. You should also open conversation about pornography. Children this age rarely seek it out but should be prepared to encounter it.

You can also talk explicitly with children this age about in-person sexual abuse. Begin with the basics, about how nobody is allowed to touch them without permission, and that asking for permission to touch them intimately is something to tell you about right away. How much more detail to get into varies from child to child. You will know best how much of this frightening topic your child can handle.

Ages 9 to 12. Somewhere in this age bracket your child will feel the earliest signs of puberty. It's a time of emotional, physical, and social change. Positivity about all three is the key point to focus on here. Lost confidence during puberty opens the door for abuse. Prepare them for the specific changes they're likely to encounter, and emphasize that they are normal, beautiful, and amazing even at their most awkward.

Though only 2 percent of youths have sex during this time, now is when to start talking about sex and sexual choices. Each family has their own moral compass about what to teach here, but every family should emphasize consent and safe sex. Circle back to where babies come from, and add what you feel is appropriate about STIs and the risks of unwanted pregnancy.

Since kids begin spending more time unsupervised online at this age, it's also a good idea to reinforce and expand on internet safety information. If you haven't already, include some discussion of sexting, nude and risqué images, and the realities of social media.

The Teen Years. Like it or not, most teenagers experiment with sex. According to research by the Guttmacher Institute, 77 percent of adults report having first had sex before their twentieth birthday, with nearly all the remaining 23 percent having had sexual contact with a partner that didn't include intercourse.

With the groundwork you've laid so far, your teen will have the basic information they need. They'll know the anatomy and the risks, and about consent and birth control. During these years, keep an open dialogue about these things in the context of teen romance and decisions about sex.

Add to this some discussion of abuse in relationships. This includes physical domestic abuse as well as those who manipulate people for sex. Help them cultivate their intuition and "gut feeling" about people and situations, so they can make good decisions.

It Gets Easier. Our culture is weird about sex. This makes it an uncomfortable topic for a lot of parents. The best advice I've seen about that is simple.

Get over it.

We're willing to take a bullet for our children, to go without so we can afford the things they want, and a million other things big and small to make their lives better. We can have a conversation that makes us blush.

And once we have that first conversation, the second one is easier. The one after that is even easier, and the one after that... until frank, open, and caring conversations about sex are just a part of being a member of your family.

52 Don't Force Affection

I have to admit it took me a while to come around on this one. After speaking with experts in psychology, communication, and defense against domestic abuse and sexual predators, I'm sold.

You've seen the narrative on social media: don't force our kids to hug relatives hello, cuddle us when they're angry, apologize when they don't feel sorry, or any other form of showing affection when they don't want to.

The reasoning for this is about consent. When we break down the costs versus the rewards, to me the answer becomes clear.

Teaching Consent Early. By the time our kids become tweens, they need to fully understand consent around physical affection. Some time in their near future, they will start to experiment with a romantic partner's body, or feel pressure to. It's our job to prepare them to make smart decisions, set boundaries they're comfortable with, and respect the decisions and boundaries of others.

When we force a toddler to hug Grandma hello, we teach them that consent about being touched is not as important as social expectations.

If we force the hug because we're worried Grandma's feelings will be hurt, we teach them that somebody's hurt feelings matter more than their decisions about their own bodies.

Fast forward to spending time alone with a partner as a teen or tween. If they've been taught often enough that their boundaries aren't worth respecting, how much they'll enforce them in that moment is pretty easy to predict.

When You Put It That Way... Having read the previous section, you'd be justified in wondering why it ever took me a while to come around on this. All I can say is that I was raised not understanding the value of my own consent.

Most of the time I wanted to hug Grandma, so it was no big deal. The times I didn't, I got the guilt trip about how she lived alone and had been looking forward to those hugs all day long.

I'm a male who grew up in the eighties deeply entrenched toxic masculinity culture. Very stereotypically, I was never put in a position where I wanted to say no. Even if I had, it wouldn't have been a situation where I couldn't physically enforce my boundaries.

But more than half the population won't have those advantages. We need to teach this early and keep reinforcing what we teach.

It took a while to get over the assumptions and programming that came from those experiences. If you dig into my Facebook, even five years ago I was posting things to the effect of "That's all well and good, but Grandma gets hugs."

I figure I'm not alone in this, so if you needed a little nudge on here...hopefully this can be it.

The Other Side. This cuts both ways. Rape culture is a buzzword in the safety and consent conversation, and has been for a while. Although I think some groups are very quick to paint everything with that brush, it's an important concept we need to combat.

Forcing our kids to show affection doesn't just teach them their own consent and bodily autonomy aren't important. It teaches them consent and bodily autonomy *in general* aren't important.

Compared to the emotions of an adult, who should be more responsible about such things than a small child, I'm pretty clear on which we should prioritize.

53 Leave Some Books Around

Fact: It's our job as parents to have open, honest conversations with our kids about sex, sexuality, and relationships.

Fact: Doing that can sometimes be uncomfortable, especially during the years our kids need those conversations the most.

Fact: The potential consequences of not having those conversations are devastating, so we need a plan.

The *best* plan is to create a family dynamic where our kids can come to us at any time, with any question, and get an honest answer without any drama or judgment. Not all of us have done that. Not all of us can do that. Even for families who did, there are cultural, familial, social, and religious aspects in play that place parts of that dynamic outside of our control.

Here's a good plan for that problem.

Leave Some Books Around. I grew up in a religious family, raised by great parents who were really uncomfortable talking about sex. I was also uncomfortable talking about personal things, and that made it harder for them to talk with me about it.

The result was that I got most of my sex education through... let's call it field research. Much of the rest I learned from sneaking peeks at my parents' copy of *The Joy of Sex*.

Every time I write about my parents, I feel the need to reiterate that they were and are awesome. I was very lucky to get the parenting I received, but every family has blind spots. The fact that I knew where they hid that book helped to fill in some of those gaps.

So I'm suggesting we do it on purpose: leave a few books out and available, or in their room, that can help them research these topics on their own, in private.

A few good books I can recommend for this:

- *Let's Talk About It*, a graphic novel by Erika Moen and Matthew Nolan. It's very frank, easy-to-digest, sex-positive, and LGBTQ+ friendly. Illustrations include nudity and can be suggestive, but not explicit.
- *100 Questions You'd Never Ask Your Parents*, by Elisabeth Henderson and Nancy Armstrong. It's exactly what it sounds like and does a good job. It's middle-of-the-road in terms of sex positivity and politics.
- *In Case You're Curious*, distributed by Planned Parenthood. It's no-nonsense and practical, covering questions from the basic to the frankly bizarre. Its main focus is on quashing the many rumors and pieces of bad information out there.
- *The Joy of Sex* by Alex Comfort. A sentimental favorite of mine and definitely for older teens and young adults. It frames sex well as an enjoyable activity people should communicate about.

I will also mention *The 7 Habits of Highly Effective Teens* by Steven Covey's son Sean. It does a great job with drilling down on teen agency and the potential consequences of sex and sexuality. It focuses too much on abstinence and scare tactics for my taste, to the point where I wouldn't use it in my house. That said, it's a good choice for families who aren't comfortable with something more explicit.

Leveling Up. If you want to take the concept to the next level, try this technique I learned from Liza Draper, who wrote the introduction for this chapter.

When her kids were of a certain age, she designated a drawer in one bathroom, in which she didn't just keep some literature about sex and sexual choices. She also kept it stocked with condoms, dental dams, and other tools for safer sex.

Her kids, and her kids' friends, knew that stuff was available no questions asked...but that she was also available to answer any questions anybody had.

I missed the boat for making such a drawer for my older son. My youngest, who is thirteen as of this writing, will have one by the time this sees print.

54 Know the Signs of Abuse and Abusers

I want my kids to have amazing friendships and romantic relationships that grow them, challenge them, and bring them joy. Once they're old enough, I want them to have great sex with partners who value them. Not everybody's on board with that last one, but that's how I feel. I want this for me, why shouldn't I want at least that for my kids?

My point is that I'm not a parent who tries to discourage their kids from getting romantic with people they feel romantic toward. I don't support abstinence-only education, and you'll never catch me trying to intimidate people who pick up my children for dates.

But Then Again... As pro-relationship and sex-positive as I am, I'm also aware that there's a lot going on with romance and sex at every age. Life-altering risks are part of that journey, and it's my responsibility to help prepare my kids for managing those risks.

I'm also aware that with relationships comes the risk of abuse. Sometimes, there can be a very fine line between sweet romantic gestures and abusive behavior. That's especially true if anybody follows the examples in too many romantic comedies.

It can be tricky to know what's going on, even without a love-struck teen making the case for somebody you're not sure about.

The good news here is that most abusers display a set of warning signs that can help you see them for who they really are.

Signs of an Abusive Personality. This isn't a medical or psychiatric diagnosis. I'm not qualified to give either. However, based on my experience and interviews with people who work in this sphere every day, nearly all abusers show a handful of traits and behaviors.

Only a few items on this list always mean somebody is an abuser, but if more than two or three show up, that's an important sign to talk with your smitten teen or young adult about this admittedly difficult topic.

- Jealousy and possessiveness
- Attempting to control time, money, behavior, clothing, eating, and other basic behaviors
- Rapidly escalating the intensity of the relationship, especially with pressure for a commitment
- Isolating, or attempting to isolate, from friends, family, and support
- Hypersensitivity, quickness to anger, and sudden changes in mood
- Consistently blaming others for their feelings and problems
- Cruelty and rudeness to children, animals, and adults in "lower" social positions
- Communicating a high degree of dependency on the partner

- A lack of friends they've known for more than a few years
- Any kind of threat or physical violence, even once
- Breaking and hitting objects out of anger
- Insisting on rigid adherence to gender roles
- A past history of abuse

This isn't a comprehensive list, but it's a good place to start. If you see these, look for other signs and symptoms both in your child and in their partner.

First Things First. Always be on your child's side. This is true in all cases, but all the more important when helping our kids manage their relationships.

This starts early, with the first relationships, well before an abuser comes into their lives. Be enthusiastic, helpful, supportive, and friendly toward their dates and partners. Root for success, however they define success in that relationship.

When the relationship ends, again, always be on their side. If they need you to be angry, be angry. Even if it was their mistake that ended the relationship. Even if you really, really liked their now-ex partner. Be on their side.

If you are always rooting for their relationships and an abuser comes along, they will be much more likely to listen to your concerns. It's no guarantee—getting an abused partner out of that kind of relationship is notoriously difficult—but it improves your chances.

55 Observe the Three Questions Rule

I have a rule I've used with my sons, a natural-consequence-slash-weaponized-honesty arrangement. It started on a spring evening when my oldest was fourteen.

There I was, clearing the kitchen counter prior to making dinner. I picked up his cell phone and the lock screen had not yet closed. On the screen was the browser, full of pornography.

It was pretty tame: just a nude woman calling attention to her nudity. My wife and I had already decided to be as sex-positive as possible, so I had no urge to punish him for his natural curiosity. But it was a teachable moment. So I showed him the screen, enjoyed the look on his face, then said…

Ask Me Three Questions. Specifically, I said something about how it was natural to be curious, but I hoped he would come to better sources than Pornhub with his questions about sex. Then I said, "Ask me three intelligent questions about sex, pornography, or relationships."

Then I shut up, maintained eye contact, and waited.

At first, he tried to stall out or refuse. Even with families who are close and open (which I believe ours is), this can be an uncomfortable topic and a weird situation. After it looked like he was going to try to get out of it, I upped the ante.

The Next Level. The next thing I said was, "Well, until you start asking questions, I'm going to talk about sex." And that's what I did. I kept it mild and informational, but definitely more detailed than a teen wants to hear from his dad just before dinner. My focus was on self-image and the expectations one might get from comparing oneself to what one sees in pornography.

It took about fifteen seconds.

His particular questions are between him and me, but I was pretty proud of them. They were honest and vulnerable. What he wondered about was the sort of stuff a kid who cares about people wonders about.

It worked well enough that we adopted the policy more broadly. It became an opener for dinner conversation, a problem-solving tool for everything from homework issues to finances, and an opening statement for other potentially fraught conversations.

We even found it worked really well as the opening salvo for potentially touchy conversations. "Ask me three questions about why I'm upset you're home after curfew" got us on the same page faster than anything else we ever tried.

Your Mileage May Vary. This has worked for us, but different families have different arrangements. The core of it, though, is important. The Three Questions Rule creates a dynamic where questions are welcomed and answered heartily with absolute candor and zero drama. It puts kids and parents on the same team, seeking information and solving problems.

Most importantly, it lays a groundwork of openness, trust, and fearlessness in the face of difficult topics, which means they'll come to us with questions for the biggest issues.

56 Invite Them to Dinner

A metric ton of studies from no less illustrious institutions than Stanford and Harvard have found eating dinner together produces numerous and wide-reaching benefits. Eating together...

- Improves children's self-esteem
- Increases vocabulary in preschool and elementary ages
- Provides opportunities to be more involved in our children's lives
- Is correlated with lower risks of substance abuse and teen pregnancy
- Leads to better communication skills
- Reduces depression, anxiety, stress, and even suicidal ideation in children and adults
- Is correlated with lower weight struggles as adults
- Encourages healthier eating habits, including a better relationship with alcohol
- Can improve the quality of our kids' adult relationships

Eating together regularly is a start, but it's not where it ends. As our children start to form friendships and romantic relationships, it's time to take the next step.

Invite them to dinner.

By "them" in this case I mean their friends when they're little. Once they reach dating age, I mean their boyfriend, girlfriend, partner, or genderfluid asexual life companion. Their BFF. Their college roommate. Everybody who's important to our children is welcome at the dinner table. So are their parents.

This can be uncomfortable. Especially if you don't like them. Extra especially if you're not comfortable with how serious or physical their relationship is. Super extra especially if you're not a particularly gregarious individual.

But It's Worth It. It's worth it because all of the benefits I listed above can apply to that dinner guest. If they stick around, it improves the quality of your extended family. If they don't, maybe that time at your table helps them live better lives wherever they end up.

It's worth it because it gives you a chance to get to know them better, which usually reduces anxiety about the influence that person has over your kids. It also helps us get to know our own kids better, since their peers and attachments are big influences as they get older.

It's worth it because over time you develop personal relationships with those friends and romantic partners. If our children's friends respect us as individuals, they are less likely to encourage our kids to engage in risky behaviors. Likewise, if things get really dicey, those friends can become our allies in helping our children make the right decisions.

It's worth it because it welcomes those people into the family. Some won't have opportunities for family dinners, and that welcome is good karma all around. Others will remain your children's friends or partners for life, in which case the earlier they feel like part of your family, the better.

Bottom line: this is a good idea. At best it shows your children that you value their friends enough to include them. At worst, it helps you keep an eye on the people who influence tweens and teens the most.

Going Further. It doesn't stop with dinner. People show their truest colors under pressure and when they're not in their comfort zones.

Many (many, many) years ago, I got invited to a family birthday party for my college girlfriend's grandmother. It was a huge gathering: family-reunion huge. I arrived several hours before she was expected. That summer I was working as a camp counselor, so I gravitated to the room where the kids and teens were playing video games.

About two hours in, I heard shouting from the other room, followed by the unmistakable sound of a punch landing. I gathered the kids and took them outside to play soccer. To this day, I'm told that woman's parents still refer to me as "Good Old Jason."

My point is that those kinds of events reveal the character of the important people in our kids' lives. Invite them to the family reunions, school plays, and the soccer games of the younger siblings. When you can afford to, bring them on family trips and movie nights.

If they turn out to be The One, it cements their place in the family. For all the others, you'll have shown respect for your child's choices while also hedging against the risks of abusive or otherwise risky friends and partners.

Plus they'll be in all those old family photos, giving you plenty of opportunities to tease them about their most embarrassing choices across the years.

57 Learn the Truth About Sexting

It's time to be very honest with ourselves. Ideally, we would like to forbid our children from sending risqué texts and photos to their partners. Many family phone agreements and house rules do exactly that.

But that's not realistic.

Expecting teens in this century to not sext is exactly as naïve as our parents expecting us to not fool around in the back seat when we borrowed the car.

I'm not saying that 100 percent of our teen children will send revealing or nude photos. I am saying that 100 percent of parents who expect a rule against it to work are incompletely protecting their kids.

So how can we help them stay safe?

New Uses for Old Tools. Although some of the risks and realities have changed, fundamentally our best line of defense for our kids is a lot like what was available for our parents.

When we were growing up, the best plan was for our parents to talk honestly and openly with us about sex. Early and often, they'd teach us about love, lust, honesty, consent, disease, protection, and how life-changing pregnancy is. They would make it clear that we could talk to or ask them about anything and keep that promise when we asked.

From my perspective, there was nothing morally wrong about us experimenting sexually in our teens. I don't believe there's anything morally wrong about a teen sending a sexual photo or text to a romantic partner.

Both are natural parts of growing up. It's just that the consequences for mistakes and bad luck regarding sex and sexting can be serious and permanent. We'd rather they wait until they're old enough to manage those risks better...even though it's unlikely that they will.

In both cases, we need to apply the best tools of education and communication with our kids. It won't be the most comfortable conversations we'll ever have, but they might be among the most important.

What Really Is New. Although sexting and fogging a car window at the drive-in are conceptually the same, twenty-first century teen sex has two important differences: permanence and propagation.

By permanence, I mean that electronic communications last forever. Even if not posted on social media, the collection of ones and zeros that compose a topless bathroom mirror photo can lurk in hard drives for decades. Forever.

By propagation, I mean how quickly those photos can spread and duplicate. A single group chat or text can put one in front of dozens of people, and that's before we start talking about revenge porn.

Taken together, there's a risk to reputation and mental health that's more intense and long-lasting than rumors about who did what with whom after the homecoming dance.

If you look at the bigger picture, this isn't such a big deal for our kids who want to be electricians, sales reps, or journalists. There are plenty of jobs where some teenage shenanigans won't get in the way of their success.

For those with an eye toward law enforcement, teaching, government jobs with security clearance, or any other profession with licenses requiring a judgment or ethics review, it can quash or derail those dreams.

Again, the best way to protect our teens from this is to teach them the risks and encourage smart decisions. We do this through communication and education from even the earliest ages, becoming more concrete and explicit as they get older.

The second best is to help them install a photo editor on their phone that includes a watermark option. For each sexual image they send, they add a unique watermark tied to the recipient. If the photo gets out, they will know who is responsible. I've heard this from a number of experts and seen it on some parenting blogs. It's good for now, with one caveat.

Watermarks are getting easier and easier to remove from photos, and there will soon be a time when they don't do much good. Maybe that time will come after your youngest child is a full-grown adult…but if not, take and give this advice with a grain of salt.

58 Don't Freak Out

The worst thing we can do when it comes to talking with our children about sex and relationships is to lose our cool.

Well, the *worst* thing would be to respond with open mockery or contempt. Freaking out is the second worst.

I think most of us see the importance of this, but sometimes not freaking out is hard. Sex and relationships are uncomfortable topics, and they carry big consequences. Between the fear and the embarrassment, most of us enter the conversation already on edge. If we get news we're not thrilled about on top of that, keeping a serene demeanor can be tricky.

So what do we do?

Practice Makes Perfect. The best approach is to prepare ourselves, by talking about tough topics early and often.

One close parallel is talking about grades and our children's future careers. This is another topic heavy with emotion and potential drama, tainted with our own unrealized dreams and worries about how they will eat food and sleep indoors as adults. Those conversations will come up years before their first relationship or sexual experimentation, and we can use them to get used to having emotionally laden conversations without emotions taking control.

This doesn't just give us a chance to rehearse, it sets up an expectation in our kids. If they know from experience that we won't freak out, they'll be more willing to talk to us about heavy topics when it comes to sex and relationships.

But What if We *Are* Freaking Out? In my experience, there are three species of parental freak-out when it comes to these conversations. There's the fear freak-out, the embarrassment freak-out, and the morality freak-out. Each species has its own solution, but the solutions for all three are ours to find.

The fear freak-out happens when our kids are making relationship or sex decisions we see as risky. They're moving too fast, and sex has life-altering consequences we don't think they're ready for. The partner they've chosen seems like an abuser, or lives a lifestyle that carries physical and economic risk. Or maybe we just don't like them.

Like any other time our fear gets the best of us, a solution is to name the fear clearly and concisely. If you're worried that your teen is getting too serious and physical too soon, lay out the specific fears: unwanted pregnancy, lost opportunities, STIs. Have a mature conversation with your teen where you talk about your fears as problems to solve as a team.

The embarrassment freak-out is more knee-jerk. Our culture is weird when it comes to talking about sex, and also weird about how we're supposed to talk to our children about sex. It's a touchy, deeply personal subject.

But as parents, it's our job to forge on anyway. A little embarrassment is worth it to maintain our kids' trust about this issue. It also models what we want them to learn. By talking about sex and relationships honestly and without drama, we show them how to talk with their partners about sex and other relationship issues. If we're weird about it, they learn that talking about sex is weird. They'll be less likely to talk with their partners the way we hope they will.

I've found two good ways to get over embarrassment when talking to our teens about this stuff. The first is practice. Talk about sex and relationships early, and take every opportunity to talk about other uncomfortable topics. By the time you get to the heavy stuff, you'll be ready. The other way is to be honest about your embarrassment. Put a verbal signpost up about how this is kind of weird. Have a laugh with your teen, then move forward together.

The Morality Freak-Out. I'm giving this freak-out its own section because it's the most dangerous. It comes from believing that some aspect of sex is wrong and bad. That might be sex before marriage, sex at your teen's age, sex between people who share genders, or some aspect of sexual identity. In some religions, even things like the position or how much you enjoy it gets defined as morally wrong.

Morals are a profoundly emotional matter, in some cases tied to religion and how well you've done your duty as a parent. That can make it very hard to not freak out if we fear our children are violating morals we hold dear.

The best approach is to remove morality from the conversation. Sex is a human function, objectively no more or less moral than eating or using the toilet. Putting too much morality on sex is what leads to teens being disowned and homeless because they're gay, or parents kicking a pregnant teenager out of the house. It's the force behind conversion therapy.

Instead, we can focus on two things. The first is the risks associated with sex and relationships, which we can handle the same way as we do our fears.

The other is to focus on the morality *surrounding* sex. Sex isn't immoral. Lying to convince somebody to have sex is. So is ignoring somebody when they withhold consent for sex. So is sharing personal information told to you in private during intimate moments. So is having sex with somebody too young, too drunk, or otherwise compromised to give consent even when they say yes. These topics are at the heart of morality and sex, while also being easier to talk about.

59 Learn the Law About Sexting

Technically speaking, a sext from a sixteen-year-old to their seventeen-year-old partner is child pornography. That escalates the potential consequences from embarrassment to serious jail time and a life on the sex offender registry. In some jurisdictions, that applies even to minors.

It's the modern equivalent of catching a permanent STI or having an early, unwanted pregnancy: a life sentence from some bad luck during a bout of youthful exuberance.

What's worse is that the law hasn't caught up with the realities. Although there is clearly a moral difference between teen loves sending each other nude photos and a pornographer victimizing children for profit, you can't count on that being reflected in the law where you live.

Teen Sexting in Your Area. Some, but not all, states have begun to update their child pornography laws to account for teen sexting. Some, but not all, jurisdictions have district attorneys who work to prevent a miscarriage of justice in cases like this.

Some less enlightened states have doubled down to confirm in court that they will treat teen sexting exactly like other instances of child pornography. The thinking there is that such draconian punishments will discourage teens from sending nude photos of themselves. I'm not an expert in law or teen psychology, but I suspect that thinking is unrealistic.

Listing the law for every place any teen might live is beyond the scope of this book. It's up to you to research the laws around sexting and nude images exchanged between teens. Once you understand them, make sure your kids understand them before the first time they're tempted to create their first one.

Also keep in mind that federal law interacts with this, sometimes in unpredictable and hard-to-understand ways. It's on us parents to understand that bit as well.

If you have the money, it's a good idea to consult with a defense attorney about this as you make your family plan. If you don't have the money, consider pooling funds with several parents you know and trust.

A Dirty Trick. Parents of younger children with internet access should know about a vicious routine some predators are using on children they meet online.

It starts with grooming a tween or younger child. Sometimes they catfish them, posing as a child their age. Sometimes they lean on a mentoring relationship. However it happens, they eventually work it up to getting their victim to send a risqué photo.

Once that happens, the predator tells their victim they just committed a felony. They say the victim created and distributed child pornography. Often they exaggerate the likely criminal sentence, as well as how horrified and disappointed the victim's parents will be if they ever find out.

From that point on, they use the threat of exposure to compel obedience from the victim. This can include financial extortion, demanding more revealing or humiliating photos...all the way up to meeting in person for physical abuse.

It's a vicious, dirty trick. And although still rare in comparison to grooming by people that families know in real life, it's on the rise.

Your best defense against this is twofold. First, like with other matters of sex and safety, talk about it early and often. Emphasize that there is no trouble your child can get in where you won't have their back. Work to keep the lines of trust and communication open.

The second is to set clear guidelines about online behavior. This should include specific warnings about common lures and tricks used by internet predators, including this one.

60 No Contact for Stalkers

If you're a parent of a teen or young adult, you have one of three relationships with stalking:

- Your child is currently the victim of a stalker.
- Your child has been the victim of a stalker.
- You are worried about your child becoming the victim of a stalker.

Serious stalking impacts about 8 percent of women and 2 percent of men at some time during their lives, according to crime statistics from the National Institute of Justice and the Centers for Disease Control and Prevention.

Light to moderate stalking, much of which goes unreported, is more common. Stalking almost never starts at a high level. It ferments. It builds up from less serious inappropriate contact, which grows if permitted unchecked.

Best Contact? No Contact. At some point during this process, there's a cycle of contact. The stalker tries to contact their victim. They call, they text, they post on social media. They show up at the office, or hang out near the car. They try to get the attention and focus of their victim by whatever means they can.

During this stage, the best response to every attempt to make contact is to not allow meaningful access. If the stalker calls from a recognizable number, don't pick up. If they call by surprise, hang up without a word. Do not respond to texts or social media contacts. If they show up in person, turn around and leave the area without any kind of interaction.

When I say no contact, I mean no contact. If the stalker leaves fifty voice mails and on the fifty-first call somebody picks up and yells at them, they have learned one thing. Unfortunately, what they've learned is that it takes fifty-one points of contact to get a response.

No matter how many times they reach out, the only response they should get is from law enforcement, a lawyer, or another authority acting in an official capacity.

It Should Go Without Saying, But... Many families have members, often male members, who feel like they should intervene with violence or the threat of violence. This is a bad idea.

Set aside for a moment the fact that assault is a crime, exposing those loved ones to criminal charges and civil suits. Forget that beating people up, or even threatening to do so, is not people living as their best selves. Ignore the psychological damage that inevitably accompanies hurting another person, even somebody you feel really has it coming. Slide right past the risk of injury to the people who offer to use violence to protect the victim. All of those are real, but there is yet another factor.

For some weird psychological reason, contact from family and loved ones of a stalking victim *counts as contact within the mind of a stalker.* An enthusiastic butt kicking from a brother or uncle scratches the same itch as hearing the victim's voice on the phone.

Bottom line: using violence to solve stalking isn't just wrong. It's wrong, it's dangerous, and it doesn't even work.

Don't Delete. You'll see advice from well-meaning amateurs about blocking stalkers' numbers on your phone and their handles on social media. The idea is the stalker will give up if you make it hard enough to reach you.

This is bad advice.

It's bad advice because it's hard to prove stalking if you have to escalate things and report to law enforcement. If you block their calls, they can't leave voice mails. If you block them on social media, they can't send messages. If you just ignore their attempts to make contact, they leave a permanent record in the form of text messages, voice mails, direct messages, and the like. You can bring that record to the police.

Sex and Relationship Safety Action Plan

General advice doesn't do much good, especially for people with free time as limited as active parents. Here's a quick checklist of the most vital action items you can start with today about safer relationships and communication about sex.

Do these this week and you're on your way to a safer family:

- ❏ Order a good book about sex and relationships and leave it in your kids' bedroom.
- ❏ Spend five minutes thinking about whether forcing affection is something your family does. If you answer "yes," brainstorm some ways to shift away from that.
- ❏ Spend ten minutes thinking about and identifying your personal "freak out points" about sex, so you can better manage them when they come up.

Find an hour soon and take action to become even safer:

- ❏ Browse your teen's social media feeds to "take the temperature" of how risqué their posts are getting.
- ❏ Look for and take advantage of your first opportunity to observe the "three questions rule."
- ❏ Set up a tools and information drawer in the guest bathroom.

Make time for these important long-term projects to become the safest family on your block:

- ❏ Invite your kids' boyfriends, girlfriends, or best friends to dinner.
- ❏ Learn the laws about teen sexting in your area. Consult with a lawyer if necessary.
- ❏ Talk, meaningfully and deeply, with your partner about creating a cohesive, goal-oriented plan for talking with your kids about sex at each age.

COMMUNICATION AND SAFETY

Introduction by Brandy Champeau

Brandy is a single mother of three children, including one with special needs. She is a writer and national speaker and runs the blog Exploring Expression, *which focuses on effective communication, parenting, and homeschooling. Find her at exploringexpression.com.*

While researching my book, *Hearing Is Not Enough, a Guide to Being a Better Listener,* I was fascinated by how simple changes in our listening habits can have significant impacts on the health of our relationships and the outcomes of situations we may find ourselves in. Considering the type of listening required in a situation, why you are listening, and what listening skills are most useful at the time is not always quick or easy but it is important. Effective communication is a skill that takes attention and effort.

Who else is more deserving of this effort than your family?

In this chapter on communication, Jason examines in depth the significance your listening and other communication skills can have on the well-being of your children and family relationships. He attacks the topic of communication from many different sides and situations while keeping hold of a single critical tenet of safety. We want to be a safe space for our children. We want them to understand that they are loved and that their thoughts, opinions, and feelings have value.

This chapter illustrates how, as parents, we can utilize effective communication tactics to build a bridge between our need to enforce boundaries and consequences and our desire to raise strong, independent young men and women.

61 Be the Shelter

The conventional wisdom is that parents are supposed to punish children when they make mistakes. That's what our parents (probably) did, and what their parents did, what *their* parents did. The only evolution was how often physical violence was part of that punishment.

"Spare the rod and spoil the child" was the go-to adage about raising good children during that era. The idea being that a healthy dose of fear kept kids on the straight and narrow until they grew into adults who knew how to act.

Add to that our own emotional reflexes, which often combine that idea of punishment with a few hours of fear that only parents with kids out later than promised know. When somebody hurts a human, it's the natural human reflex to hurt back. To lash out with words, with punishments and restrictions. That's an understandable reflex, and one our society has supported and enforced for many generations.

But what if I told you there was a better way?

A Newer Approach. When our children screw up, they are usually asking questions. Some of the big ones include:

- Who's in charge here?
- What will it take to get some attention?
- Can I do this easy thing instead of the hard thing?
- How can I deal with these angry, frustrated, or scared emotions inside of me?
- Why can't I do what I want all the time?
- Will my parents still love me if I do this?

That last question is the most important and is usually being asked along with all of the others. The answer is, of course, YES... but when we respond to their screw-ups with anger and arbitrary punishment, we cast some doubt on that answer.

The other thing that happens when our kids get caught screwing up is that they're already having a bad day. They know they're in trouble. They might have already gotten a serving of discipline and disapproval at school. They walk in the door at home emotionally bruised because they've spent the day in a storm.

It's our job to be the shelter in that storm. To greet them with unconditional love, comfort, and a space to just relax into the outcomes of their bad decisions. To know for certain we are on their side even when they're being knuckleheads.

Once our kids have come home, been reminded they are loved, and had a chance to recover from the day, it's time to have the conversation. To talk about the realistic consequences the world imposes for making the mistakes they just made. To discuss how those consequences will impact their life at home and how their behavior impacts the people they love. To work out how we can help them deal with those consequences with maturity and grace.

A Matter of Sides. It often feels like kids act out as a way of scoring points in a game only they are playing. As parents, if we can always be on our children's side, they won't feel as much need to score points against us.

It's a shift in mind-set for many parents. Moving from "Boy, are you in trouble" to "This is a problem. Let's solve it together" isn't what many of us were taught.

This shift is powerful. In so many chapters of this book, I underscore the value of our children knowing they can come to us with anything. They have to know that when we learn about their problems, our first instinct will be to help them find solutions. If they instead think our first instinct will be to add hardship and punishment to the problems they already have, how likely will they be to rely on us?

It's not such a big deal when the problems come from cheating on a math test or skipping school. But what if the problem is a boyfriend who's overly aggressive about sex? Or a teacher or coach who makes them uncomfortable? Or an adult threatening to blackmail them over a risqué photo they sent?

Life teaches consequences soon enough and hard enough. It plays for keeps, and it plays dirty. We can impart and reveal the meaningful ones while remaining a point of safety and shelter.

62 The Sword of Insertion

Interrupting is rude. It increases the chances of a misunderstanding because part of a thought gets cut off. It raises the level of stress and tension in the conversation by speeding the tempo and creating conflict. Maybe worst from a parenting point of view, interrupting our kids tells them we don't respect them, their thoughts, or their words.

On the other hand, sometimes it's important to interrupt. Usually, this happens in one of two circumstances.

Situation #1 happens when you're up against a timeline. You need to be at school/church/the game/the play/the airport in an hour, which means everybody has to be in the car ready to go in ten minutes. So of course your child chooses this moment to start a lengthy argument. They might even have a valid point, but there isn't time for the conversation right now.

Situation #2 happens to adults and children, especially under stress. Venting and talking about problems often helps but can also spiral upwards. Each sentence uttered about a hot topic makes whoever's speaking angrier and angrier as they engage more deeply with the emotions around what they're talking about. You know from experience that what needs to happen is for that person to just stop talking for a few minutes, but because they're in this verbal feedback loop, they're not going to do that on their own.

Incidentally, this also happens with drunk people, people on drugs, and people in emotional states that bring them into contact with police. Many police are trained in the de-escalation system of Verbal Judo, which is where this technique comes from.

If you're in a conversation with your kids, or anybody really, and you have to interrupt, the Sword of Insertion is a sentence you can use to interrupt successfully while showing respect at the same time. Here it is:

"Let me make sure I understand what you just said."

Lead in with "Hold on" or "Wait a second," and hold up one or both hands, palms outward. Follow up with the Sword of Insertion: "Let me make sure I understand what you just said."

If you do this with respectful body language and voice tone, it stops the momentum of the conversation. It tells your child you care about what they're saying. It demonstrates respect for their thoughts. *And* it gives you control over where the conversation goes next.

For best results, where it goes immediately is to you restating the main point of contention. When you restate it, you can use calmer voice tones, more effective word choice, and more relaxed body language. Since you're restating it honestly and with love, your child's emotional state will usually become more productive, too.

If you're in Situation #1, you can get the day back on track. Acknowledge the issue that has your child upset, commit to solving the problem together soon, and get their agreement that now is not the time.

If you're in Situation #2, you can get the conversation back on track. Acknowledge their feelings, reframe the disagreement as something you can work on together, then sit down and talk about it in a productive way.

The Verbal Judo folks call this the "Sword of Insertion" because they come from a law enforcement/military/warrior mind-set and those guys like weapon metaphors. You can call it whatever you like.

When It's Time to Listen. For parents (myself included) who have a habit of interrupting, try this simple trick that combines active listening and mindfulness meditation.

While your child, partner, friend, or coworker is talking, just breathe. In through your nose, out through your mouth. Focus on their words and your breath, and wait until they've finished expressing their thoughts fully. This little exercise will make you more present and attentive, and has the bonus of giving you time to fully formulate your own words before they slip out.

63   Be Respectful About Fears

Being a parent is scary. This whole book is about things that scare parents. Our observations and intuition about danger are two of the most powerful tools we use to keep our families safe.

But if we focus on those things, we're missing a really important point: What scares our kids?

It's vital to take our kids' fears seriously, even when those fears are ridiculous or largely imaginary. These conversations are our first chance to teach our kids that we will listen and help find solutions when they're worried and to model what to do about the things that frighten us.

Professional bodyguard Spencer Coursen tells a story about a client's child. While he was protecting the family, this young girl developed a fixation about wolves living in her closet, in a high-rise apartment, in New York City.

Admit it. You just laughed a little bit.

That laughter is natural but can be devastating to a frightened child. Instead of mocking her or tuning their daughter's fears out, the family spent a week helping the child research the habits and habitats of wolves. On her own, the child reached the conclusion that penthouse closets aren't a likely place to encounter wolves. She put her own fears to bed and became more informed and empowered in the process.

If we establish this dynamic early, we raise problem-solvers: kids who know how to address fears and do something about them.

More important, we raise kids who will come to us with questions and fears about teachers, coaches, bullies, sex, drugs, mental health, and similar problems as they get older. They will never be afraid to talk with us about fear because they know we will always be on their side.

It starts small, and it might start silly, but we have to start on the right foot.

Active Listening. Active listening is a way of hearing people that both makes sure you get a complete picture of what they're saying and shows them, through what you say and do, that you are listening.

Because kids often get used to not being listened to by adults, active listening can be incredibly powerful for them.

You can take whole courses on this skill, but for now keep the following concepts and early practices in mind:

- Use attentive body language like nodding your head and maintaining eye contact. Demonstrate that you are listening by listening with your whole body.
- Ask open-ended questions to encourage further details. This draws out information and shows that you care about more than just the surface facts.
- Paraphrase or summarize what you've heard to show that you're listening and that you want to get it right.
- Use occasional positive reinforcement, interjecting about how you understand, or that you're proud of your child for bravely sharing.
- Avoid anything that would make your child feel rushed. It's easy for them to interpret that as you becoming bored or impatient with what they're saying.

If we apply these concepts to conversations about our kids' fears, it shows them how seriously we take their safety and their emotional well-being. Later on, they'll remember this, not just about their fears, but also about their hopes, dreams, crushes, and suspicions.

64 Look for the Why

Conflict is part of parenting, whether we're trying to convince a toddler to use the potty, a grade school student to turn off their Xbox, a middle schooler to do their homework, or a high schooler to admit they borrowed the car without asking.

You and your child will not always agree on everything, and you will come into conflict.

There are a lot of different approaches to conflict with our kids, and different people can have different opinions in good faith.

That said, every family communication expert I spoke to had some variation on the same advice.

Whatever you're arguing about with your child isn't nearly as important as your child knowing you are always, *always* on their side.

One way to accomplish this is to enter every conflict by looking for the why.

It's Like This. When your arm hurts, you won't heal it by just treating the pain. That's a symptom, but not the problem. You will heal it by finding out if you sprained your wrist, got stung by a bee, or developed tennis elbow.

If you sprained your wrist, no amount of bee sting ointment will help. You're solving the wrong problem.

When you're in conflict with your children and don't understand the why, you can end up arguing about the wrong thing. A conversation you think is about grades, but your teen thinks is about having time with their crush, is a hard conversation to succeed in.

Where to Find the Why. Sometimes looking for the why in conversations with tweens and teens can feel like playing *Where's Waldo* while somebody's moving the picture.

This is another topic that could fill an entire book, but based on my interviews with experts ranging from hostage negotiators to school counselors, here are some places to start:

- Listen actively so you can pick up on which things in the conversation bear the most emotional weight for your child.
- Paraphrase what your child says to make sure you focus on the right things.
- Remember your child's most common triggers and emotional anchors, and think about how they interact with the conversation at hand.
- Approach problems as a team, working together against the trouble. Watch what solutions your child comes up with.

- Avoid using authority whenever possible. It tends to shut down communication and build resentment.

Once you've identified the underlying why of any conflict, you are much better able to solve that issue and work together with your child.

Look at Yourself. Finding the why works both ways. You might be escalating a conflict yourself, or working at cross purposes with the other people in the conversation.

An example most parents of teens can relate to is when your child comes home after curfew. On top of everything else, you've spent some hours worried about your kid, imagining the worst. Those emotions and their accompanying neurochemicals have been doing a number on you...and now that your child shows up unconcerned, the conversation can very quickly go sideways.

But if you identify the fear, you gain power over it. You can control it better, and you can help your teen understand that your fear for their safety is a big part of why curfew is important.

In real time, or ideally before you begin the conversation, ask yourself what you are feeling and why you are feeling it. Those questions can help you find the why for your side of the conversation. Armed with the why for yourself, you can pre-empt any unhealthy or unproductive things you might do or say and have a better conversation overall.

All that's left then is to figure out how you and your child can both get what you need.

65 Rehearse Important Conversations

What if I told you that you already practiced a habit that can help you communicate more effectively and affectionately with your kids?

I hope you'll be okay with that, because it's exactly what I'm about to do.

The Fine Art of Shower Arguments. You know those times when you're in the shower, thinking about a confrontation you had or are going to have. The next thing you know, you're running through some imaginary version of it.

Sometimes it's all in your head. Other times it's out loud, echoed beautifully in the stunning acoustics of your shower stall.

Or in your car. Or the treadmill room at the gym. Shower arguments happen all the time. Even if you're one of the rare people who never engages in them, you know somebody who does.

This basic human impulse is something you can put to work to have better conversations with your loved ones.

Beginning with the Goal in Mind. There is one basic difference between a shower argument and what I'm suggesting here.

Most shower arguments don't have a specific goal. They're a form of venting or a fantasy left behind when the water turns off. We're letting off steam about something we're mad or nervous about.

But what if we had them with the goal of rehearsing how we will have an upcoming conversation with our kids? What if we went through what we would say, and how we would respond to their most likely counterarguments?

What if we even let ourselves go off for a bit, really putting our frustrations out there, so we didn't have to when our kids are present later?

Imagine a situation every parent of teens goes through at least once. Your teen is hours late after curfew and you haven't heard from them. You've spent those hours imagining horrific scenes of car accidents or worse. You're scared, and scared is a short hop from angry.

When your teen arrives safely, that anger comes out. You don't mean for it to, but it ambushes you both and the conversation goes poorly.

What if you spent some of those hours rehearsing the conversation? You get to vent that fear and anger, saying the things you mean in the moment but shouldn't say out loud. You get to fine-tune what you'll say and fill it with the love and mutual respect it should have.

Your teen gets home, and they're expecting a blowup. It's not like they didn't know what time it was. Instead, they get your polished, edited, honest thoughts. The conversation goes well. Everybody wins.

Avoiding the Rabbit Hole. Sometimes when we vent, like in a shower conversation, we let out a lot of anger and frustration. We feel better when it's done.

Other times, we spiral upward in our frustration. Every sentence attaches to and builds up further resentment. We end up angrier than we were in the beginning. It's even worse if this happens when we're talking with our loved ones. Things get out of hand rapidly, and we end up saying things we really shouldn't and don't mean.

If we practice those hard conversations ahead of time, we can beat that rabbit hole in two different ways.

Sometimes, our own mental health needs the rabbit hole. We spiral up until we're frothing, but once we're done we don't need to do it again. We can move forward with a productive mind-set and have the conversation the right way.

Other times, we can repeat the rabbit hole as many times as we find it, but rehearsal helps us identify where it is. We locate our triggers, practice dodging around them, and rehearse what we'll do to stay out if our kid tries to push us in.

In both cases, we stay out of it when it matters.

66 Use Jedi Mind Tricks

Between adults, manipulation is bad. It's disrespectful, dishonest, sometimes passive aggressive.

On the other hand, your personal trainer manipulates you with strategic compliments to keep you inspired. If you go to therapy, you're manipulated every session in one way or another. To me, a lot of it comes down to intent. Is the manipulation to help somebody, or to hurt somebody, or to gain power? Some reasons make it good. Others make it bad.

No matter how you feel about manipulating adults, every parent needs some simple manipulations in their communication toolbox.

A great example doesn't work so well for parents but is a lifesaver when managing groups of children. If one kid acts out, don't call them on it. Half the time they're doing it for attention. Calling them on it is giving them attention.

Instead, pick a nearby kid and compliment them for doing what you want. The other kid sees what it takes to get attention, and you seal the deal when you compliment them soon for doing right.

If you're ever in a position to do so, try it. You will be amazed.

Like I said, that one's not really appropriate for most parenting situations. Here are a few Jedi Mind Tricks that are.

The Car Ride Trick. Many of us took car rides with our infants and cruisers back when something about being in the car seat and out for a drive put them directly to sleep. It was another Jedi Trick, though not really of the mind.

For older kids, even our adult children, there's something about talking while taking a drive together. It reduces distractions, creates an unconscious sense of shared purpose, and seats you in positions that minimize the power imbalance between parent and child. It also makes eye contact less of an issue, since you're watching the road.

Having a Catch. If you came up in a ball sports family, you spent time in the backyard throwing a ball back and forth with one or both parents. That repetitive action done together often drifted into some of the best conversations of your childhood.

It doesn't have to be throwing and catching a ball. Any shared activity can be that catalyst, as long as it doesn't take too much concentration or coaching.

For example, my sons and I do it over home improvement projects. It works with painting or hanging drywall, but not for wiring a new electrical outlet. Also, it works better now than when they were younger and I spent most of that time teaching them construction skills.

Other parents did it under the hood of a car, while hiking, or across a chess or Risk board. The specific activity doesn't matter. It's the vibe and opportunity that activity creates.

What if You Did? Has any parent in the history of parenting made it through the teenage years without learning to hate the sentence "I don't know?"

It's a showstopper, unconsciously intended to avoid the effort of continuing a conversation.

Sometimes we should acknowledge that our child just isn't feeling a family chat right now. That's okay, and we should respect their autonomy when we can. Other times, that simply won't work.

In those situations, respond with, "What would you say if you did know?" Wait for an answer, but don't let them off the hook.

A Quiet Voice Is the Loudest. It's natural, almost reflexive, to raise our voices for the most intense and important things we have to say. It's also a bad move.

When somebody raises their voice, the other people in the conversation raise theirs. They talk faster and take defensive (or aggressive) postures. Listening becomes second priority.

But what happens when you're in a conversation and can barely hear the other person? You lean forward. You tune out distractions. You focus your efforts on hearing what they have to say. You *listen*.

Orators, interrogators, and salespeople use this trick every day. There's no reason we can't use this power for the good of our families.

67 Begin with the Goal in Mind

This is a classic, stated in just this way by Stephen Covey in *The Seven Habits of Highly Successful People*. It's the second of the seven and up front for good reason. The book was written for business use initially, so seeing it in action is easy within a business context.

Imagine a team tasked with designing a book cover. If everybody went to different offices and made a cover, they would come back with wildly different ideas. Though that creativity can be a plus in some circumstances, it doesn't work with a tight budget or timeline.

Before separating for brainstorm sessions, the team would do well to first set goals about the size, color, basic content guidelines, font style, and audience for the book. With the goal of creating that sort of cover in mind, they avoid wasting time while they work. When they come back together, everybody has created some variation on the essential theme of a cover.

In the book, Covey applies this to our personal lives, so our motion toward our goals creates actual progress. Here I want to suggest we can apply the same concept to communicating with our kids.

I'm not saying their goals and ours will always be the same. I'm suggesting we should make sure what we say and do is in line with what we want the conversation to accomplish.

What Does This Have to Do with Safety? I'll throw out a few examples.

Some young jerk is cursing your family and threatening you in a road-rage incident. Is your goal to protect your ego, to teach him a lesson, or to get home safely?

You've had maybe one too many drinks but you're under the legal limit. Is your goal to get home with the convenience of driving your own car, or to get home as safely as possible?

Deciding on a password for your home network, is your goal to make it easy for the family to remember? Or is it to keep criminals from hacking your Wi-Fi security cameras?

You get the idea.

Beginning with the end in mind is especially important when having those harder conversations with our kids because it's especially easy for those conversations to go off track.

They might veer off because our fear is bigger in that moment than our rational assessment of danger. They might go sideways because our kids know how to push our buttons. A lot of things can push those talks off course, but beginning with the end in mind can make it harder to do and easier to get back on track.

So It Begins... In my experience, those most vital talks with our kids work best if we begin with the goal in mind across three stages of the conversation.

Before things start, set the goal. Decide ahead of time what you want to learn and communicate. Take a breath, solidify your intent, and start off on a foot that serves what you want to accomplish.

During the talk, remember the goal. When emotions rise, or interesting side topics pop up, or your child throws out a wickedly observant insult, step back to the goal. Steer away from what doesn't serve it, and lean in to what does.

At the end of the talk, circle back to the goal. Ask yourself if you've attained it or made enough progress in that direction. For older children, ask them if they think you've done the job.

We're doing Mr. Covey one better: begin, conduct, and end these conversations with our goals in mind.

68   Take Five When You Need To

I don't know who needs to hear this, but you have permission to step back from a conversation when it's getting out of control.

Or you're getting out of control.

Or your kid is getting out of control.

Or you're both getting out of control and the worst sides of yourselves and your emotions end up running the show.

The best parents in the world end up in arguments with their kids where people say mean things they don't mean. When that happens, it's natural and easy to flare up and make everything worse.

We can stop that by simply giving ourselves permission to leave the conversation. Gently, lovingly, but firmly, we can take a minute to reset ourselves.

No. Really. It's Okay. Taking five (or ten, or however long you need) when things get heated does a lot for communication with our children.

- It removes the possibility of us retorting with something hurtful.
- It means the teen who's acting up can't keep saying hurtful things to us.
- It lowers the tension in the room so emotions and arguments can reset.
- It shows our children that we care more about our relationship with them than about winning an argument.
- It models a healthy way to handle heated conflict with the people we love.

To be clear, I'm not suggesting storming out with an expletive and a slammed door. I'm not talking about throwing a guilt trip at our children then cutting off conversation, or sending them to their room, or putting any blame or onus on them.

We need to take it on ourselves. Use language like, "Wow. I need a minute. How about we go do our own things for a while, then come back to this in ten?"

That way, we're not accidentally doing something passive-aggressive that hurts our kids. We're communicating our needs clearly, lovingly, and respectfully.

The Safeword. Many marital counselors recommend using a conversational safeword that pauses a conversation. If either partner uses the word, the subject comes off the table for an agreed-upon period.

In some cases the conversation can continue, just not about that topic. In other cases the couple needs to take a break from each other entirely.

Either way, the agreement is to respect the pause button absolutely, so people who need a break can get a break.

You might consider setting up a pause button word with your children for everybody to use if a conversation is getting out of hand. It can give you an out and show your children how much you respect their emotional needs.

69 Listen for the Language of Depression

Depression and anxiety are on the rise among teens, tweens, and even younger children. According to data from the National Survey of Children's Health, incidences of both among children ages three to seventeen increased by 50 percent between 2015 and 2020.

Harm from anxiety and depression is increasing alongside it. Similar research has found corresponding rises in suicide, suicidal ideation, and self-harm behavior like cutting and eating disorders.

What can we do?

I mentioned in the Golden Rules about not being therapists. We aren't qualified to provide professional-grade mental health care. But we can watch for early signs and get our children in a room with professionals as soon as it will help.

It's Not Just Being Sad. The way we use the English language is not always consistent. For example, the word "bad" can mean anything from "I don't like that," to "It's morally repugnant," to "That person is good at fighting," to "I like that."

That applies to some key words when discussing mental health. We sometimes use the word "anxious" to mean nervous or afraid. We sometimes use the word "depressed" to mean sad. In both cases, we're referring to emotional states that aren't just normal, but sometimes necessary for growth and mental health.

But also...

- "Anxiety" can mean a medical condition defined by excessive feelings of worry and fear that impacts wellness and can overwhelm other thoughts.
- "Depression" can mean a medical condition causing persistent or excessive low moods, lack of energy, or loss of interest in people and activities that usually bring joy.

Mistaking the first usage for the second is bad, but mistaking the second for the first can be lethal.

Again, only a qualified professional can tell the difference, and sometimes only after extensive observation and testing. One of the best ways we can determine if our child needs that observation and testing is to look for the language of depression and anxiety.

The Language of Depression and Anxiety. That term isn't exactly accurate. We're not looking for any particular words or vocabulary here. Instead, we want to be alert for ideas our children express that indicate certain states of mind.

Depression often expresses itself with…
- A strong preference for negative words over positive words
- No longer bringing up favorite topics
- Indicating a lack of joy from things that usually made them happy
- Placing more than proportional blame on themselves when things go wrong
- Speaking more quietly or slowly than usual
- Expressing a sense of helplessness in the face of obstacles
- Expressing a sense of hopelessness about life in general

Anxiety often expresses itself with…
- Irritability in conversation
- Anger that seems disproportionate to what caused it
- Refusing to speak or hesitating in the middle of sentences
- Reticence to commit to easily attained goals
- Not wanting to participate in activities
- Complaining of secondary symptoms like headaches, stomachaches, and sleep issues
- Reporting or indicating worrying and negative thoughts

In both cases, one incidence of one item on the list doesn't indicate clinical depression or anxiety. Instead, look for patterns. Multiple items, or just one or two showing up consistently, can mean it's time to speak with a professional.

Like I mentioned in the Golden Rules chapter, be especially alert for change. If a child is normally cranky, that might not indicate anxiety, but if they change from irritability to compliance that might mean something big. Likewise for a teen who is constantly talking about dark subjects and is otherwise perfectly fine but slowly stops deriving joy from their horror novels and death metal music.

70 Know Your Own Buttons

I have a photo I cherish.

It's of me and a woman named Sharon Meyer. Sharon and I co-taught the classes at American Kenpo Karate Academies at their flagship school for most of the late 1990s. She outranked me and was a little younger than my parents. We worked together closely every day, and I've long called her my "mom away from mom."

In the photo, taken on the training deck, she's looking at me with this very parental expression balanced perfectly between amusement and exasperation.

I don't remember what I did to deserve that look, but I love that it was captured for posterity.

Though she was more amused than annoyed in that moment, it could have been worse. Nobody knows how to push our buttons like our kids.

But Here's a Secret. When a teen pushes our buttons, what is their goal? It's not really to hurt our feelings. Well, that's not the real goal. It might be their immediate intention, but that's just a side effect.

A teen going on the offensive is usually after one thing. They want to stop having whatever conversation you're in with them.

They might be afraid you'll punish them. They might be embarrassed or anxious about the topic. They could just be bored or wishing they were doing something else. The reasons change, but the goal is almost always the same: they want the conversation to end.

If they get to you, usually one of three things happen. They can derail the conversation completely and make you change the subject. They can push you to blow up so the conversation is now about how you shouldn't yell. They can get you to talk about their disrespect.

In all three cases, did you see what's not happening any more? You're not talking about whatever you were discussing before they pushed your buttons.

Taking the Power Back. We have all earned our sore subjects, weak spots, and chinks in our armor. They're real, and our friends take care not to poke us in them.

Our children aren't our friends. We own those buttons, and it's our responsibility to not respond when they get pushed. How to get there is different for every parent, and sometimes for every different situation, but it's on us to get there.

Sometimes it can help to think about the buttons our kids are likely to push given the talk we're about to have. We can push those buttons ourselves until we're temporarily immune to them. Sometimes it can help to meditate or take some deep breaths before the conversations, so we enter it harder to rile.

It's even fair to respond to a button push by taking a break from the conversation, like I suggested earlier in this section.

Owning our buttons gives us the power in confrontation with everybody, including our kids. After all, we need to remember who's the grown-up here.

Communication and Safety Action Plan

General advice doesn't do much good, especially for people with free time as limited as active parents. Here's a quick checklist of the most vital action items you can start with today about making communication a safety tool instead of a safety hazard.

Do these this week and you're on your way to a safer family:

- ❏ Attempt the "Sword of Insertion" once this week when disagreeing with your kids.
- ❏ Try lowering your voice when your child raises theirs, and note what happens.
- ❏ Before your next potentially fraught conversation, take five minutes to rehearse it in your mind.

Find an hour soon and take action to become even safer:

- ❏ The next time you're in conflict with your child, look for the "win-win" solution and put both of you on the same side.
- ❏ Create a conversational "time out" signal for your family to use when conflict gets too heated. Pair it with a set plan for returning to the argument when everyone is feeling more resourceful.

Make time for these important long-term projects to become the safest family on your block:

- ❏ Talk with your co-parent about what questions your children are asking when they engage in behaviors you would like to see change. Get congruent about the answers and how you will share them.
- ❏ Take some time for a week to journal about the times your kids have really gotten under your skin. Keep an eye out for patterns that reveal specific "buttons" you can take time to work through.

SECTION 8

TRAVEL SAFETY

Introduction by Andrea Leschak

Dr. Andrea Leschak is a pharmacist turned patient advocate and travel health coach. Frustrated by people feeling dismissed and overwhelmed by the healthcare system, she empowers clients as the founder and CEO of Wayfinder Advantage. She performs individual and group coaching, workshops, and keynote presentations. Find out more at wayfinderadvantage.com.

"Listen. I can't *find* your mom," my husband told me. "You stopped to look at something. I told your mom to stand at the street corner and wait for me. After finding you, I retraced my steps, and she was gone."

I looked at my husband. He was in the military then, and little rattled him. Yet, I could tell by the tone in his voice that he was serious.

As we rushed down the crowded streets, I replayed the past few hours in my mind.

My mother *had* been acting odd. She was a seasoned traveler but seemed more confused and hadn't adjusted to the time change. I thought her behavior was a combination of jet lag and the long-term effects of high-dose chemotherapy from her prior cancer treatments.

Thoughts of "What was she wearing? Did she have her passport? How *do* you describe a fifty-plus-year-old woman from Tennessee to the Belgian authorities?" ran through my mind.

Worse still, we hadn't created an "if we get separated, let's all meet here" plan. And why would we? We were hardcore travelers, and we had *never* been separated like this.

We scanned the crowd, hoping to catch a glimpse of her. It was bitterly cold, so we thought she might have stepped inside a shop to stay warm and got distracted. We selected a few of the most enticing stores and went door to door.

Relief! We found her, wrapped in her puffy coat, happily looking at tea sets, oblivious to our concern.

This scary moment illustrates why this chapter is essential reading for all travelers. Jason reminds us that travel safety is rooted in planning, honing traveler self-reliance, developing situational awareness, and setting boundaries.

71 Watch the Three Factors of Family Travel Safety

I'm a big fan of travel. It grows us as people, even when we're adults. Travel for children can be life-changing for their outlook, their confidence, and their belief in what they can experience and achieve.

I'm also a big fan of planning correctly for family travel safety. This can seem intimidating at first, but really family travel safety starts with just three questions.

Question 1: Who's Going? There's a short answer and a long answer to this question. The short answer is a list of everybody coming on the trip with you.

The long answer covers the abilities and needs of each person on that list:

- What skills relevant to travel does each person have?
- What skills relevant to your destination does each person have?
- What kind of physical condition are they in?
- Do any of them have a temporary or chronic illness or disability?

- What special needs does each person have—for example, a wheelchair or access to specialized medication?
- What age and stage of development is each at?

You get the idea. Each time we travel, we assemble a team whose task is to have a great time while staying safe. You're creating mini-dossiers on each team member.

Question 2: Where Are You Going? You already know the name and general location for your journey. This question digs deeper. You'll want to look specifically at:

- What kinds of activities are you likely to do there?
- In what ways does the location present more risk compared to where you live? For crime, weather, pollution, accidents, and personal vulnerabilities?
- What level of medical care is available, and how do you access it?
- How are the police? What is their response like when dealing with tourists?
- What laws and customs do you need to navigate around while there?
- How common is your native language at your destination?

Some of this information is easy to find online. For others, you might need to call some contacts or reach out to local information sources. In a later chapter, I've written about a few online resources that can help you with this.

Question 3: What Will You Do? The final question is to ask what kind of activities you plan on engaging in.

This starts with brainstorming and researching the activities available at your destination. Compare your list with the needs and abilities of your team. Each activity ends up in one of four categories:

1. Everybody can do it, no problem.
2. Most people can do it easily, and one or two need accommodation.
3. Only some of your team can do this safely.
4. Nobody on your team can do it safely.

Categories 1 and 4 make the decision easy. It's a clear yes or no, no further questions asked.

For category 2, ask what accommodations people need and who will be responsible for providing them. For example, you want to do a wilderness hike and one family member has insulin-dependent diabetes. They will need emergency sugar or glucose just in case, and somebody needs to watch them for early warning symptoms. With both in place, you should be able to safely do the activity.

For category 3, you have two choices. You can forgo the activity since it's not safe for everybody, or you can split up and do two separate activities on that part of your trip.

Divide and Conquer. It's smart to do this more than once. Start with looking at your destination in general, then do it again for your specific destination each day.

On a week-long trip to Thailand, for example, the answers for two days in Bangkok will be different from the next two days on a river cruise. Likewise, a trip for the whole group will have different answers from a day when you split up for separate activities.

Ideally, you will have done some version of this for each day and major activity of your trip. It doesn't have to be some kind of formal report like a bodyguard would create for a corporate client. Just some notes on paper can be enough.

72 Put on the Security Blanket

So there I was, in Kuala Lumpur with my wife and my sons aged four and fourteen at the time. We were there for the Thaipusam festival, a religious holiday where more than a million people flock to the holy shrine at the Batu Caves. There was a lot going on: crowds, pickpockets, brutal heat, a long wait in line on a steep staircase, managing bathroom breaks, holding our place in the queue…keeping it all in my head was exhausting.

Even though nothing bad happened, both of us were out of it by the time we reached the shrine, and utterly done when we got back to our hotel.

The security blanket method would have helped us. We would have been safer while also enjoying the experience much more.

Squad Tactics. Our problem there in Kuala Lumpur was that both of us were responsible for every aspect of our family's safety the entire time. That's a huge task, and even bigger at such an enormous event. It drained us completely.

When bodyguards prepare for an assignment, everybody on the team gets a specific task. Though they understand how their task interacts with other team members, they focus on their task alone. The man assigned to handle radio communications doesn't worry about driving the car, and the driver doesn't try to keep a hand free to draw their weapon.

Some of these plans, especially for high-risk assignments, are complex. They rely on elite training and specialized equipment. They're great for presidents, celebrities, and CEOs. They're unnecessary for an average family taking in the sights.

There is a plan that's perfect for families like ours: the security blanket.

The Security Blanket. I first heard about the security blanket from bodyguard and bodyguard teacher Tom Patire. I think the term is his, but it's an adaptation of standard squad tactics for protection agents.

With the security blanket, each of two parents is assigned the job of "Security" or the job of "Blanket."

- **Security** is responsible for safety factors outside the family. Security watches for traffic, predators, and pickpockets. They watch the weather and tell people to watch for the rough patch on the sidewalk.
- **Blanket** is responsible for safety factors inside the family. They corral the kids and keep them within arm's reach. They watch for signs of heat exhaustion and hypothermia, distribute snacks, and reapply sunblock.

Between the two roles, all bases are covered. This works well for a traditional two-parent family, but with even a little tweaking, it can work for most family constellations. A single parent might deputize the oldest child as Blanket. A multigenerational family might need to put a teenager on Blanket to also watch an elder who's no longer as capable as they once were. Families travelling together might subdivide the roles between multiple adults or rotate through the two roles over the course of the day.

Parental Rest. The other thing bodyguard teams get is relief personnel. As shifts go on, new people come to fill them so team members can rest and stay alert. Parents traveling with their kids don't have that luxury.

Our off-duty time comes back at the hotel room, in a space where our kids can get on their phones behind a locked door. In a pinch, a parent can take on all duties while the other takes five in the restroom or at a café table.

Security Blanket can give you the next best thing, by swapping with your partner every so often. It's not full relaxation, but changing what we're responsible for is the closest thing to rest parents often get.

73 Watch the Locals

The exciting thing about travel is seeing new places and new cultures. It's why we travel. It's especially why we want our kids to travel, so they can experience that diversity and variety and grow into more open and sophisticated adults.

But that same variety presents parents with a safety challenge. We don't know the rules in places we visit. We don't know what behaviors mean trouble. We don't know what clothes say about a person or which phrases are a bad idea. We don't know which neighborhoods, restaurants, or events are safe. If something goes wrong, we often don't even know who to approach for help.

And that's before we even begin dealing with the language barrier.

The best solution to this is to go to places where you're familiar with the culture and the language. The second best is to visit places where you know somebody so they can guide you. Not everybody has either option for every place they want to take their families. Besides, only going places you're already familiar with goes against the whole point of travel.

So what can we do instead?

Your On-Site Security Team. Do you know who understands all the rules, signs, signals, and weird bits and pieces of how to stay safe in any place in the world?

That's right: the people who live there.

When we're in a place we're not familiar with, we can learn much of what we need to know from the locals. For example:

- Compare how they dress to how you're dressed. In open countries, this can give you a lower profile. In restrictive and conservative countries, this can save you from harassment or even legal trouble.
- Listen to how loudly they speak, and at what cadence, so you can tell if your voice or somebody else's is showing aggression or dishonesty.
- Check how many locals are in restaurants you're considering. They're a good gauge of food quality and safety.
- Try to notice who locals steer clear of. What do they have in common? Certain modes of dress? Tattoos? A way of walking?
- Do they pay cash or use credit cards most of the time? How carefully do they handle cash when out in public?
- How closely do they watch their children?
- Are there places or times they behave differently than the norm? What do those places and times have in common?
- What body language do they use when negotiating? When approaching a stranger? When apologizing?

At the most basic level, if we keep our travels and explorations to places lots of locals spend time, we will be in places with lots of witnesses. Most criminals avoid witnesses. Pickpockets can be an issue in crowds, but crowded spaces can protect us and our children from violent crime.

Getting Active. There's also a lot of benefit from asking locals directly for help and advice. Start with the manager or concierge at your hotel. They get paid in tips and are motivated to keep guests happy. Although some get a small kickback for recommending a restaurant or bar, those recommendations are likely to be safe. At worst you'll be overcharged.

Other locals who can help you include cab or Uber drivers, local law enforcement, restaurant owners, shop owners, and tour guides. Research these ahead of time, since they're not always reliable. In some destinations, cab drivers or police are corrupt. In others, shop owners will take advantage of any tourist who seems like they don't know what they're doing. Find out who you can trust, then ask them for what you need to know.

74 Learn the Local Scam

Lonely Planet publishes country, region, and even city guidebooks for most destinations on the planet. Before the internet, they were the go-to resource for travelers who wanted smart, detailed information about where they wanted to travel next.

In the 90s and early 2000s, when I was traveling without the benefit of the web, I noticed that every single book had at least one paragraph about local scams. When I went to Beijing, it warned me against taxicab touts in the airport, who would offer rides to town at three to four times the going rate. My first trip to Puerto Vallarta, the guide went into detail about timeshare scams from local con men and from real time-shares with terrible deals. The guide for Siem Reap gave hints on how to tell the difference between a massage parlor and a "massage parlor," if you know what I mean.

I've mentioned before that I don't give much advice about property crime because I want to focus on the most important things. However, especially in places where you don't know the customs or speak the language, what starts as a mugging or con job could quickly escalate to an assault or worse. It pays to know what the local scams are.

I still buy the *Lonely Planet* guides for places I visit. They make better casual reading than websites, plus they make nice souvenirs when I get back home. But *LP* is only one of the resources I use. It's not even the one I trust most, since things might have changed by the time the volume in my hand was printed.

Every Town Has One. Well, more than one. But it seems like anyplace you go has one special common scam that's unique or at least favored among the local wildlife. So buy the guidebook, check the location profiles from the government resource of your choice, watch the Facebook groups, and hang out in the expat forums. Identify it.

First, it protects you from that particular scam. You know what it is and how to recognize it. You develop a plan for stopping it early and often. Knowing about the Beijing taxi touts, I knew to walk past them to the actual cab line and pay a reasonable fee. Understanding the Puerto Vallarta timeshare situation got me several delicious free meals for the cost of a little bit of my time.

Second, it puts you in an aware and empowered mind-set. That mind-set will impact how you move when you reach your destination. That confidence and power deters criminals considering that and other scams.

Don't stop there. Beyond the colorful local pastime, every location has a wide spectrum of scams and crimes, some specifically targeting visitors. The local scam is your starting point.

The Big Time. In some parts of the world, the local "scam" is actually a violent crime. As of this writing, Mexico, Venezuela, Columbia, Haiti, and South Africa all have high incidences for kidnapping of visiting tourists. North Korea, Iran, and Russia put visitors at risk of government abuse and detainment.

Just in case it needs saying, those destinations belong off our travel bucket list while our kids are still young. They might have been a great adventure back when we had fewer responsibilities, and they will remain a possibility once our children are grown and established as adults. For now, though, there are plenty of interesting, challenging, and safer places to travel with our kids.

75 Count in the Bathroom

Keeping a low profile is an important safety skill everywhere, but especially when you're traveling. The problem with this when you leave the country is that keeping a low profile is tricky when you're not from the area.

A person from the developed world who can afford foreign travel is unfathomably wealthy in comparison with the local population in many popular tourist destinations. Between that and how you look, move, and dress differently, you will attract attention while you're abroad with your family.

This book isn't about protecting your stuff. It's about protecting your kids. I wouldn't mention pickpockets and quick scams, except that sometimes those situations get out of hand. When they get out of hand, people get hurt. Your first and best line of defense against that is to not make yourself an attractive target to begin with. One of the best ways to mess that up is to count your money where people can see it.

Here's an easy way to avoid doing that.

While you're out and about in foreign places, keep your money in three places. Most of your cash should stay secured in your hotel: bring only twice as much as you think you'll need for any given outing. Of the cash on hand, keep a small amount in a front pocket: enough to handle any simple transaction like paying for a meal or buying a souvenir. The rest you keep hidden in a money belt or a secret pocket, or pinned inside your clothing.

When you need to count your money or move it from your hidden cache to your front pocket, don't do that in public. It defeats the purpose and draws attention from exactly the wrong people.

Instead, go to the restroom. Lock yourself in a stall. In that private space, pull out your reserve cash and replenish your front pocket fund.

The same goes if you need to count your money. Go in the stall. Put your backpack, purse, or whatever on your lap as a work surface. Count everything, then redistribute to your pocket and your hidden cache.

Doing this does protect you from pickpockets, but it also means you're not flashing a wad of cash where more violent criminals might see it. You're already a bigger target than you are at home whenever you travel. This lowers your value to local bad guys by not making yourself look even more attractive.

One Last Little Thing. This hack comes from Jim Alsup, a real-deal secret agent who has the best advice for drawing less attention while in exotic places.

As soon as you can after arriving, head to a local store. Not a tourist trap, but the equivalent of a Walmart. Buy a hat, a shirt, and a pair of sunglasses in the style you see locals wearing. These don't just give you protective coloration. They provide cool keepsakes when you bring them home.

76 Learn What Drowning Looks Like

On TV and in the movies, people drowning always make a big scene. They splash, yell for help, and carry on in ways people around them can't help but notice. That's when the hero dives in and rescues the almost-victim. Very often, most of the people involved are wearing a lot less clothing than you would expect for that situation.

But that's TV, and the dress code is only one part of how it's different from reality.

Because few of us see people drowning in real life, we're programmed for the experience by what we see in shows. If we're on the lookout for loud, splashy, visible drownings, we're looking for the wrong thing.

So many family vacations involve time in and around the water, even if it's just a few hours at the hotel pool. Since that's true, it's important for parents to know what drowning really looks like.

The Sad Truth. Human beings, even small human beings, are hard-wired to stay alive. That means, when the body thinks it's at risk for drowning, it tries everything to stop that from happening.

By the time somebody reaches the point of actually beginning to drown, they're exhausted from their attempts to get to safety. They don't have breath to shout. They don't have the strength to wave or splash. They slip under the surface quietly, and once they're under you can't see or hear them until it's too late.

Even before that time comes, the human body has an instinctive drowning response. Unless trained to do otherwise, we will tilt our heads back and wave our arms and legs beneath the water. This saves energy, but also makes a drowning person harder to see and much harder to notice among a group of other swimmers.

These are both really awful images, especially if we're thinking about our own children when we picture it.

But now you know what drowning looks and sounds like. Which means you are better able to prevent drowning than you were a couple of minutes ago. The best way to prevent childhood drowning is to always have an alert, sober adult on site whose sole job at that time is to keep an eye on all the children in the water.

I recommend doing this in shifts, with each adult watching for twenty or thirty minutes at a time. Fatigue won't set in so the adult on watch's mind doesn't wander, and nobody will miss out entirely on whatever the adults are doing for their own fun.

What You Can Do. Swimming lessons are your children's best line of defense against drowning after they reach an appropriate age.

While we're on the topic, when was the last time you took a swimming lesson? Are you a strong swimmer? If so, are you strong enough to get to shore from a lake or river? Are you strong enough to do that while towing your child? Are you a strong enough swimmer to do that while injured?

Whatever your swimming level is, there's always a class or some practice you can do to get better. The better swimmer you are, the safer your children are in the water when you're around. It's not the most adventurous or glamorous skill to improve, but it can be one of the most important.

If you're a super-strong swimmer, take a look at some water rescue courses. Knowing how to swim and knowing how to save a drowning victim in open water are two very different skills.

77 Use Online Tools for Safe Travel Planning

Advance is a trade term used by bodyguards and other protectors. It means the work done before a client arrives someplace, to make sure that place is safe. When you have a big budget (think a country's president or a billionaire), you send a team several days ahead to check everything out.

Most parents don't have that kind of budget. But we can use the concept, and some of their best tools, to prepare for our trips and make them both safer and easier. Here are my top five online tools to help you do that.

Smart Traveler. This is the Australian government's public information for travelers. Each country listing includes detailed information about crime, health care, travel advisories, and any important major differences in the local laws.

The US State Department also maintains a similar site. I like Australia's better because, over the twenty years I've been using both, Australia's seems less influenced by the politics of whoever's in charge at the time. (Or I just don't see the influence because I'm less familiar with Australian politics.)

Use this site when you're choosing destinations, and again once you've made your choices. It gives a strong overview of the safety realities you will meet when you get there.

Google Maps/Google Earth. You know what this is, and what it does. But you might not know how useful it is for safe travel planning.

Once you know where you're going, you can use this to locate various places you'll visit: hotels, museums, tourist attractions, etc. After you use the maps app, switch over to Google Earth. Use both the satellite and street views to get a good sense of what the destination and route look like. You will be surprised how useful those details become, even if it's just so you'll recognize buildings and other landmarks while getting there.

Although this is the best app available to civilians for this kind of planning, it won't necessarily be useful to you once you're in-country. Breakups in signal and phone functionality will sometimes kill this app. For real-time information on site, you'll use Waze (see below).

Safe-xplore. The only for-pay app on this list, Safe-xplore gives you a personalized travel risk report with suggestions. The professional version, Safe-esteem is used by protectors several thousand times per day.

When you put in your information, it gives you a weighted report that outlines property crime, violence, accidents, environmental issues, and health concerns as compared to your home and other potential destinations. It also offers personal profiles for travelers with specific concerns like women traveling alone, LGBTQ+ travelers, and people with medical conditions.

Waze. You already have at least one map and route app on your phone, but you should use Waze for two reasons.

First, it's the most popular app of its kind once you get out of North America. That means it reliably works most places you'll want to travel.

Second, it aggressively crowdsources real-time reports of things like accidents, police checkpoints, and bad road conditions.

All put together, this is the winner for your navigation while you're in-country. Whether you're driving yourself or checking the cab driver's work, it is reliable and accurate in a way that most other apps are not.

911 by Country. For only about 20 percent of countries in the world, 911 is the emergency services phone number. In the UK it's 999. Vietnam uses 113. Russia, 102. Google "911 by country" to find one of several solid lists. Find the number(s) for your destination(s) and put them on the back of your phone with a label maker, sticker, or marker.

Expat Forums. Run a Google search for "[Place You'll Visit] Expat Forums."

Expat stands for "expatriate," which means somebody who has left their own country to live someplace else…usually somebody from an English-speaking nation.

These forums are populated by people who live where you want to go, and who know the details like any other local plus the particular hazards of being a foreigner in that region. The conversations on these forums are specific, detailed, and honest. There's no better source for the real-deal intel about a destination.

78 There's Always a Door in the Kitchen

Every spy movie, emergency plan, and tactical advice video on YouTube tells you to know where the exits are whenever you enter a room or building.

It's good advice. If you come in someplace, you should know two ways out of that place. This works when you're home. You know your house, your friends' houses, your kids' schools, your church, and the places you visit regularly. You've thought about fires and other situations and come up with an escape plan, even if only subconsciously.

This falls apart when we travel, because by definition we're going to places we're unfamiliar with.

If we're traveling to more exotic locations, we're not just unfamiliar. We're in a place where exit signs might be in another language, or entirely absent.

In conversations with bodyguards who have kept clients safe all over the world, I learned this simple fact that all the professionals know and use.

There's Always a Door in the Kitchen. Restaurants worldwide have an exit door in the kitchen. They have to bring in food deliveries and take out trash. Staff needs to slip out for a smoke.

Even where building and health codes don't require it, you will reliably find a way out through the kitchen. When you enter a restaurant or bar, watch for where the food servers come from. That's your path out in an emergency.

In some places, especially hotels and convention centers, the kitchen exit might lead first to a service hallway. That's okay. Just follow it and you'll get outside soon enough.

Improvise, Adapt, and Overcome. If you're escaping from a fire or similar disaster, you can find the kitchen and run through it to the outside. Nobody will yell at you for entering the private areas of the building under those circumstances.

If you're escaping from some kind of criminal event like a robbery or shooting, kitchens are still your best escape route.

I want to be clear. The best plan in a criminal event is to escape. Run through and out of the kitchen just like the building was on fire. This is especially true in places where you don't know the law or the local criminal hierarchy. Just escape.

But if you can't escape for some reason, kitchens are a good place to hole up. They're full of heavy machinery to take cover behind and well-stocked with things you can turn into weapons. Knives, heavy pans, boiling water, meat hammers, spray bottles of industrial cleaners…all sorts of ways to ruin a bad guy's day.

A Matter of Convenience. One more reason the kitchen exit is good to know about and use: the staff uses it too.

In a lot of countries with fewer safety laws, and even in developed countries where it's illegal, sometimes the rear exits end up unusable.

Businesses often use the emergency exit spaces for storage, blocking the door with pallets of drinks or cleaning supplies. In high-crime areas, the owners sometimes chain the doors closed to prevent criminals from coming in the back way.

You can't always rely on the emergency exits actually providing an exit.

That kitchen exit, though. That's the one the staff uses to bring in supplies and take out the trash. It's where they talk to their friends and slip out for their breaks. With the exception of the customer entrance, it's the one where the staff has the most motivation to keep clear and working.

There's always a door in the kitchen. Remember it. Look for it. Incorporate it into your emergency plans.

79 Take a Morning Photo

When a child gets lost on vacation, they almost always return safely. They just got lost or separated, and no predator or criminal took them. It's scary for parent and child alike, but in the end there's no real harm done.

That said, imagine for a moment being in an unfamiliar city or foreign country when you turn around and can't find your child. Your first search doesn't find them, so you find a police officer. They ask you what your child looks like.

While deeply afraid, you struggle to remember details of their height, hair, build, and clothes on that particular day. Even if you remember exactly right, as opposed to yesterday or the day before, you then have to find the words to communicate that. If you're traveling overseas, you might also have to overcome a language gap. And all this time, you are losing vital seconds that could be spent searching for your child.

There's a simple solution, and you already carry it with you.

At the beginning of each travel day, take a photo of each child. Make it a celebration. Make it funny. Play up the doting parent who wants to record every special moment, even setting out for the next day in your family travel adventure.

Chances are, you'll never need that photo. If your child does get lost, when the manager, security guard, or police officer asks what they look like, you just bring up the photo and point to it.

In most cases, you can text it to that person, who will then text an up-to-date image of your child to everybody in their network. It takes seconds and is 100-percent accurate.

80 Observe and Respect the No-Go Line

Here's an important fact about family safety, especially family travel safety, we all need to keep in mind.

When you make a plan sitting comfortably at home at the table with a beverage nearby, safe and warm, you are smarter than you will be when you're implementing the plan in the field.

Think about the last time you were in full family vacation mode. You were tired. You were a little confused. The kids had been clamoring for attention/trying to get themselves killed/asking for money for a few hours. You were probably dehydrated. You might have had your "dad goggles" on, where you focus on a short-term goal even though nothing but that desire suggests it's really all that important.

There's no real replacement for information on the ground, and sometimes we find the reality of a situation is so different from what we thought it would be that we have to change the plan. Most of the time, though, if we did our planning well, that's not the case.

This is especially important when things start to go wrong because travelling parents often end up in the following cycle:

- **Step One**: Have a plan for the day/afternoon/location.
- **Step Two**: Things start out all right.
- **Step Three**: A small thing goes wrong.
- **Step Four**: That small thing begins to cascade into either multiple small things or one big thing.

- **Step Five**: Because we've already mentally committed to the plan, we keep moving forward instead of stopping to reassess.
- **Step Six**: At best, we all have less of a good time than we could have. At worst, somebody gets hurt.

A no-go line, decided on ahead of time and agreed to by everybody on the trip, saves you from that process.

No-Go Line Basics. A no-go line is exactly what it sounds like. Before you set off, either at home prior to leaving or in the morning before the day's events, you think deeply about the activity you're going to do.

Look for places things could get sketchy. Note locations that could be a problem, hazards associated with that area, potential equipment failures, and similar problems. Think about who's coming with you and what might go wrong with each of them while you're traveling.

Based on that thought (and any research you need to do), you set up an "If A, then B" statement, where B is always either aborting or significantly changing your plan.

Here are some examples:

- Going on a desert hike: "If we get to less than a pint of water each, we turn around and go back."
- Swimming at the beach: "If the tide gets above that line of rocks, we pack it in and go home."
- Going dancing while visiting a town you don't know well: "If we see more than one young man drunk, we go home immediately."
- Visiting an amusement park in the middle of summer: "If anybody looks dehydrated, we find shade and rest for half an hour."

You get the idea. A no-go line helps you set the rules for your trip while you're still in your right mind.

The Most Likely Problem for a No-Go Line. No-go lines are an excellent tool for family travel safety, but they have one serious flaw. They only work if you respect them.

Take the desert hike example. When you reach that point where your group has less than a pint of water each, it will be tempting to say, "But it's only another two miles! We've got this!" But remember in that situation that your planning self was smarter than your doing self.

This is a simple concept to understand and easy enough to practice in the planning stages. It's harder to implement in the moment, but hey…we're parents. We had to turn in our "do stupid things" license the moment our first baby met the world.

Travel Safety Action Plan

General advice doesn't do much good, especially for people with free time as limited as active parents. Here's a quick checklist of the most vital action items you can start with today about safety while you travel.

Do these this week and you're on your way to a safer family:

- ❏ Register your family with the STEP program at the US Department of State, or its equivalent if you live in another country.
- ❏ The next time your family goes on any kind of expedition, try the "morning photo" trick to see how quick and easy it is.
- ❏ Install WAZE on your phone.

Find an hour soon and take action to become even safer:

- ❏ Discuss the "Security Blanket" with your co-parent and try it the next time your family goes out.
- ❏ The next time you go out to eat, play a game where everyone in the family spots the exits. Compare notes to see if anybody missed one.
- ❏ Make a list of items your family absolutely needs when they travel. Keep it somewhere on your hard drive or cloud storage so you can print it before every trip, no matter how hectic the preparations are.

Make time for these important long-term projects to become the safest family on your block:

- ❏ Create a mini-dossier about each of the people you travel with most often. Include their strengths, weaknesses, and any special requirements they might have while out and about.
- ❏ The next time your family leaves for an unfamiliar destination, spend a few hours on Facebook groups for locals of that area.
- ❏ Talk with your co-parent about each other's blind spots while traveling, and use them to set up default no-go lines for when you travel.

EMERGENCY PREPARATION

Introduction by Erika Friday

Erika Friday is a mom-life coach who helps families gain more happiness, peace, and ease through a combination of mind-set and skill set. With the motto "prepared and present," Erika teaches emergency preparedness, household management, and fulfillment as a parent and person. Find more at readysetmoms.com and on Instagram at @readysetmoms.

Earthquakes, wildfires, blizzards, power outages, injuries, and other medical emergencies come to mind. The sorts of things that are out of our control. If much of this book is about preventing emergencies, this chapter will help you prepare for and respond to them.

I'm sure you'll appreciate Jason's realistic, level-headed approach to emergency preparedness. He helps you envision the different scenarios that might require you to shelter in place or evacuate, and what you'll need to know, do, and have.

Instead of putting all your time, attention, effort, and money into "an emergency kit," you'll be led through communication, developing a plan, stocking your home, stocking your first-aid kit, and more.

81 Build a Communications Tree

A communications tree was originally a list of phone numbers. When news had to spread, the person at the top of the list would call the person in the second position. The second position would get the news, then call the third person…all the way down until everybody knew what they needed to know.

New technology has made that model obsolete. Mass texts, email blasts, and group chats mean that one person can notify everybody in just a few more seconds than it takes to notify one person.

That doesn't mean you don't need an emergency communications tree. It's just going to look a little different.

Modern Solutions for Modern Times. The challenge with emergency communications in the modern era isn't reaching people. It's making sure they get the message in our time-crunched, stimulation-overloaded life. Our focus isn't on disseminating the information. It's on confirming key people have received it.

For example, imagine an emergency that means your child needs to get picked up early from soccer practice. It's not enough to drop a note to your partner that you can't do it. You have to know they have received the message and are on the case.

A communications tree helps make that happen. When it works, you can be certain the communications part of your job is finished so you can focus on the next tasks needed to keep your family safe.

The Five Ws of Communications Trees. Each participant in a family communications plan needs to know the following things:

- **Who** they are responsible to contact.
- **What** information they must relay.
- **When** they need to get that information to them.
- **Where** (by what means) they will communicate.
- **Why** the information is important.

One way to put this together is by starting with a list of people you need involved in an emergency. This might be a general list for all emergencies, or you might have different lists for different situations. For each person, determine their key task.

Some people will have linchpin duties, like picking up children and elders and bringing them to a safe location. Others, like an adult child living in another state, might only be responsible to let people know they are safe and sheltering.

Once that list of people and duties is complete, create the communications tree. Assign each their five Ws, then run through it once to make certain nobody is left out.

A modern communications tree ends up looking more like a web, but the concept remains the same.

Achilles' Heel. Modern communications trees have lots going for them, but they have a serious vulnerability. Major emergencies often come with a side order of lost connectivity, lost electricity, or both. As you put together your communications tree, consider also developing back-up plans for times when cell phones and the internet don't work.

See the chapter on PACE plans for some thoughts about that.

82 Look for the Helpers

Children's television icon and very probably saint Fred Rogers once gave this advice to children who see something awful on the news:

"When I was a boy and I would see scary things in the news, my mother would say to me, 'Look for the helpers. You will always find people who are helping.'"

It's great advice for kids. It comforts them and gives them something less awful to focus on. It reinforces the idea the world is mostly good and filled with good people. Which is true.

It's great advice for us too.

With a Caveat. In 2018, a writer named Ian Bogost wrote a piece for *The Atlantic* about how Mr. Roger's advice was bad for adults. Mr. Bogost was undeniably being a buzzkill, but he also had a point.

As parents, we can't just look for helpers. *We are the helpers.* We're the helpers our children are looking to for reassurance that the world is good and safe. If we look to others, we miss opportunities. Sometimes those missed opportunities can lead to tragedy. It's on us.

That was the point of the *Atlantic* article, but that point also misses the most important part of Mr. Rogers's message.

We Can Still Look for the Helpers. As parents, we are the helpers. I think we all had that moment, early in our parenting years, where we found a problem and looked around for the person responsible to fix it…and realized that was us.

But we need a team. That's what looking for the helpers means for parents.

Before emergencies happen, we can build a list of people who can help us. People to call when things go sideways. People we can learn new skills from. People we can make part of our circle because they're good in the right moments.

During emergencies, we can reach out to those helpers. They might be friends and community members we know will come through in the clinch. They might be professionals we call to the scene. They might be innocent bystanders or nearby strangers we loop in for extra hands, eyes, and minds.

After an emergency is over, we still need helpers. People to clean up the mess. Counselors, doctors, and therapists to help manage the trauma. Friends to debrief with, gain comfort from, and plan with for the next time.

These helpers can keep emergencies from becoming tragedies. We need them, and they need us to be their helpers.

The Diffusion of Responsibility. You've heard the story of Kitty Genovese, even if you don't recognize the name right away. This twenty-eight-year-old woman was stabbed to death in New York in 1964. Two weeks later, a sensationalistic news article claimed this happened while neighbors watched from windows without offering any help. Even though the account shows up in criminology and psychology textbooks, the truth is much less grim. The court and investigatory documents show that she was far less visible, and that people rushed to her aid when they saw her plight.

So that's good news, but the urban myth does illustrate a phenomenon that really happens.

Sometimes you need to create helpers on the spot. You might be tending your injured children after a car accident and need somebody to call 911. Another person might think they are being stalked and need a stranger to walk with them to their car.

When that happens, don't say, "Somebody call 911," or "Can somebody walk me to my car?" or any similar phrase. Studies have shown that rarely gets results. Diffusion of responsibility kicks in. Everybody who hears you assumes somebody else is doing it, so it never gets done.

Instead, point to somebody. Get their name. Use their name to give them specific instructions. Ask them, "Can you do that?" then move on when they give you a yes. If there are enough people, assign two or three people to each task.

That's the best way to create helpers when none are around.

83 Stock Your Home Without Going Overboard

The CDC recommends keeping enough emergency supplies on hand to last your family at least three days. Leading experts on preparedness recommend two weeks or more.

If you filled all your buckets and pots and dug all the way to the back of your pantry, how much food and water could you gather if things broke down? How long would your medical and communications supplies last? For most families, the answer is a couple of days at most.

Don't panic. One trouble with advice on emergency preparedness is that the people giving that advice tend to be...extreme about it. They're picturing the End of the World as We Know It. They even have an acronym: EOTWAWKI. They truly believe "Winter Is Coming." (Please ignore the preceding reference if you've never seen *Game of Thrones*.)

Reading their blogs and watching their videos, it's easy to feel like anything short of an underground bunker is insufficient.

By some standards, that level of preparation would be ideal. If everybody had enough emergency supplies to make it through a month-long or year-long breakdown of services, we would all be safer. But that's a serious project, and a lot of us lack the money, the time, even the space in our homes for that to be realistic.

But every family can gradually, in less than a year, stock up those days or weeks of emergency supplies so they're on hand for everything from a two-day blackout to the week and a half after a major storm.

What to Do Instead. Let's look again at that CDC recommendation. Three days is as long as most local and regional emergencies last. We're talking about winter storms that close roads and down power grids, hurricanes that flood neighborhoods, and earthquakes that hit urban areas.

The immediate shock and tragedy are real. The damage and cost can be long-lasting and severe. But the breakdown of services rarely lasts more than a few days in the developed world. If things aren't back to normal, local and national resources will deploy and provide the things you don't have.

So start with three days. One you have three days, it's easy to expand that to a week, then two. In most places, prepping beyond two weeks means prepping for the EOTWAWKI. That's a different animal.

How do we get to those first three days?

Stocking Your Home Step by Step. Even if you're pressed for time or tight on money, you can stock minimal supplies over a few weeks with these easy steps.

- **One**: Count how many people live in your home. Add anybody likely to shelter in place with you.
- **Two**: Multiply that number by ten meals, three gallons of water, and one package of sanitary wipes.
- **Three**: Each time you go shopping, add two meals' worth of simple supplies like canned food, rice, or beans. Pick up a pack of bottled water and one package of sanitary wipes.
- **Four**: Take the extra supplies home and store them someplace out of the way.
- **Five**: Repeat steps three and four until you've stocked to the result of step two.

Once you get your three days set, consider keeping it up until you're set for a month or more.

A Word about Rotation. Eventually, even canned food goes bad. Water, too, because plastic degrades and microorganisms can enter the containers. Once you have your emergency supplies stocked, use and replace them as recipes require. For example, when you make chili for the big game, buy all the cans of beans you need for the recipe. Use the cans in your emergency supplies and replace them with the cans you buy.

This takes getting used to, but you'll be surprised how little it really requires.

A Few Durable Items. Consumables are the key factors in preparing for an emergency. That said, your supply cache will do much better with a few additional tools:

- Flashlights with extra batteries
- An emergency radio
- Charging blocks for phones
- A well-stocked first-aid kit
- Manual can opener
- Signal whistle
- Dust masks
- Work gloves

For any of these you don't have, add one to each shopping trip until you're fully stocked. You can go even deeper on emergency equipment than you can on consumable supplies, but this is an excellent start.

84 Three Kinds of Go Bags

If you Google emergency preparedness you will eventually end up on the subject of "go bags." Some of it is useful. Some of it is grossly commercial, with a generous side order of fearmongering.

Let's talk about preparedness bags without the fear, without the sales pitch, and without that vague sense that people are sort of hoping to need them.

Go Bag Basics. The purpose of a go bag is to collect all the things you will need for an emergency in one place so you can grab it and take it with you when the time comes.

You can go deep here, building an array of well-stocked bags for every conceivable occasion. Most of us can get by with at most three different bags.

- An **underbed bag,** for middle-of-the-night emergencies
- An **everyday carry kit**, for keeping with you all the time
- A **boogie bag**, for when you have to leave in a hurry

Underbed Bags. None of us are at our best when we wake up in the middle of the night. We're even less at our best when what wakes us up delivers a healthy dose of fear and adrenaline. Underbed bags collect necessities for the next few hours if a disaster comes while we're sleeping.

An underbed bag should contain:

- Your second-newest pair of shoes, with socks stuffed in them (or your third-newest if you've put a second pair in the car)
- Flashlight with extra batteries
- Signal whistle
- Bottle of water

- Protein bar or similar portable nutrition
- One day's worth of time-sensitive prescription medication (if needed)
- Spare glasses (if needed)
- Underlayer clothes or a windbreaker

When woken up in an emergency, you can't go looking for all these items. Just keep them under the bed in a spare bag. I like those totes people keep giving away free these days. When the time comes, scoop up the tote, get out of the house, and use the supplies as needed.

Everyday Carry Kit. EDCs are immensely popular among the conceal-and-carry community and other tacticool types. You can spend a lot of money buying one ready-made or a lot of time custom building yours. That's what a lot of gloriously bearded men on YouTube recommend.

Those manly types forget that the Mom Purse is the ultimate EDC kit. It's not a Batman-style utility belt stocked with weapons, hemostatic bandages, and a flashlight bright enough to stun a charging grizzly. It doesn't need to be in an ankle holster or weigh eight pounds.

It just needs to be easily portable and hold the stuff you need. For most of us, that's a small boo-boo kit, a flashlight, a pen knife or multitool, and a granola bar. Add a space blanket, phone charger, and some paracord if you want to get super-fancy.

Even with a simple kit, how to keep and carry it becomes a question. Women, and men secure enough to carry satchels, have a simple solution. The rest of us can distribute the gear in multiple pockets, invest in an ankle or belt EDC holster, put on a fanny pack, or get over the idea that purses are just for women. It's the twenty-first century.

Boogie Bag. You'll also hear these called "get-out bags," "bug-out bags," and similar. I heard "boogie bag" once and liked it, so that's what I'll call it here. This is your larger emergency kit, stocked with a few days' worth of survival gear to get you from where you are to where you need to go in an emergency.

Spy movies show these all the time: a dramatically black duffel stuffed with cash, spare passports, ammunition, and some other toys and tools. If you need that kind of boogie bag, I recommend you reassess some of your recent life choices.

For the rest of us, start building a boogie bag by choosing where it's meant to take you and under what conditions. Do you need to get to your parents' house two counties over? The school you work at, which is a designated emergency staging point? A hotel just outside of town to wait out a fire or flood? Do you just need to get home from work?

Based on that information, you will know how much food or water goes in your boogie bag. You will know what tools and other supplies you'll need. Once you have the list, gathering the supplies and putting them in a durable, comfortable backpack won't be difficult.

85 Build an Emergency Plan

When emergencies happen, our bodies and brains flood with neurochemicals built to keep us alive but which also reduce our ability to function in complex situations.

The most effective solution for this is long-term, intensive stress inoculation training like they give to secret agents and Navy Seals...but that's neither appropriate nor realistic for most of us.

The second most effective solution for this is having and rehearsing a plan.

This works because it bypasses decision-making skills during the key moments. As things go sideways, and neurochemicals essentially get you high, all you have to do is remember the plan.

Doing that takes far less of your higher-order thinking skills, which means you can still do it while loaded up with adrenaline.

The Elements of a Plan. You've made plans before. As a parent, you've probably gotten pretty good at it. A working emergency plan defines:

- What emergency is happening
- Who will be involved
- What risks are posed to those individuals
- What action each person will take
- What equipment and skills are required
- Who will come to help
- Who will communicate with the help, and how
- When the emergency is defined as over

This may feel like a lot, but in many cases it's fairly simple and intuitive. Imagine a child breaking their leg at the park.

- The emergency is an injured child.
- The child, their younger sibling, and a parent are involved.
- Only the injured child is at risk, and the risk is worsening the injury.
- The parent will administer first aid while the sibling calls EMS.
- The plan needs a cell phone, and basic first-aid skills from the parent.
- EMS ambulance services will come for help.
- The younger sibling will call EMS using the parent's cell phone.
- The emergency is over once EMS arrives and takes over.

That's probably the way things would go for your family even if you didn't create a plan about it. All creating a plan does is make sure that the parent and sibling remember their tasks in that stressful and frightening moment.

Creating a Plan. The best plans are created in times and places far removed from when they come up. If you're comfortable and safe, your higher-order thinking works well. You have the right brain for creating a plan.

I recommend sitting down from with your co-parents (and later with your tweens and teens) and creating simple plans for the most likely emergency situations.

A few of the most important include:
- Injured or seriously ill family member
- Child lost in public
- Attack or attempted attack while the family is in public
- Car accident
- Car breakdown
- Child being bullied
- Fire in the home
- Encountering somebody who needs help
- Natural catastrophes common in your region

Some of these you can group into categories, with the same basic plan for two or more emergencies. It's easier to memorize three or four plans than a dozen or more.

Plans and Young Children. The most common pushback I hear about creating emergency plans is fear of scaring young children. People who put this forward are usually worried that bringing up the possibility of a problem puts the idea in their kids' minds.

I am not a child psychologist, but I have been working with children in self-defense and safety for over thirty years. In my experience, by the time a child can understand the explanation of a danger, they have already thought about that danger on their own.

If we talk with them about dangers in the context of creating a plan, fear becomes knowledge. Worry becomes empowerment. They see their parents are making plans to keep them safe, that we have their back, that they can take personal action to help keep themselves and the family safe.

As long as you keep the descriptions, and their assigned roles, age-appropriate, they will be just fine.

86 Use Social Media for Emergency Communications

When things go wrong, local phone networks become unreliable. People in the area call each other. People from outside call to see if they're okay. Officials and emergency responders coordinate.

It's important to communicate with our families during emergencies, but our cell phones aren't the best tool for the job.

Even without damage to the networks, the lines are unreliable for our purposes…and we're using bandwidth better used by people trying to bring help to where it's needed most.

Calling a loved one during an emergency only works if they're available to take that call at the exact moment you manage to get signal and work through the overcrowded network. Then you have to keep that signal long enough to talk.

On top of that, the conversation isn't likely to be on point. You will both be emotional, and communicating the most essential safety information will take longer than you think.

There is a better way.

Use Social Media. As compared to cell phone calls, social media has a lot of advantages in an emergency:

- It doesn't use the cellular networks (assuming you're on a computer, or set your phone to Wi-Fi).
- Internet service tends to be more robust than cellular service.
- The major social media platforms are built on an international scale, insulating them from regional breakdowns.
- You can post a message and leave it there, where loved ones can view it when they're available.
- It's easier to communicate key safety information via text than with voice.
- You can post photos and videos to convey precise information.

Although they've been caught misbehaving lately, Facebook is the best tool for this. They're established, robust, backed up, and easy to use.

The best recommendation here is to set up a private group chat via Facebook or the Facebook Messenger app. Use it for day-to-day chat and coordination, and make it known that it will also be the communications hub in an emergency. WhatsApp is another good platform for this.

87 Create PACE Plans

Emergency management teams and the military have a saying: "One is none. Two is one."

It's about how having one piece of essential equipment leaves you in bad shape if it breaks, gets stolen, or gets dropped off the side of a boat. The acronym PACE expresses a powerful approach for this.

PACE stands for:

- **Primary**: What you use for this task by default.
- **Auxiliary**: Your usual second try if the primary doesn't work.
- **Contingency**: What you go to next.
- **Emergency**: A new modality if normal channels have completely broken down.

An Easy Example. Imagine a teen who needs to reach their parents. Their Primary method would be to use their cell phone and call them. Their Secondary (maybe their phone's battery is dead) would be using a nearby friend's phone.

If neither of those work, the Contingency might be using a land line wherever they are. As an Emergency measure, like I mentioned in the previous chapter, they could leave a message on a family internet chat room.

Equipment, Skills, and Knowledge. To carry out a PACE plan in real life, anybody participating needs some equipment, skills, and knowledge.

In the example above, the Primary needs the teen to have a working phone. The Secondary and Contingency plans need the teen to have memorized their parents' phone numbers. The

Contingency also relies on the presence of a land line wherever the teen happens to be. The Emergency measure requires a set-up group chat and knowledge of how to log in to it.

There are two ways to build a PACE plan that accommodates these factors. One way is to build each step, keeping in mind the gear and capacity of the people who will carry out the plan. The other is to make the plan, then equip and train the people involved to suit.

The first is easier. The second grows your family's emergency readiness more quickly. It's up to you which works best for your family.

Going Deeper. Let's make another example of a PACE plan, one that's more robust and used in more serious straits than calling home during school. Imagine getting home from work during an emergency.

The Primary is driving home using the regular route. The Secondary, for if major roads are closed or packed with cars, would be to drive home via a secondary route.

The Contingency plan comes into play if the car isn't operable or if all roads are closed or clogged. In a town with commuter rail, that might be a good choice, since it often avoids heavy traffic. If the parent is fit, they might borrow a bicycle to get home. The Contingency might even be sheltering at the office, or in a nearby friend's house, until the situation has passed.

The Emergency measure is simple and drastic: walking home, no matter how long that journey is.

Let's Not Go Overboard. Once you get started with PACE it can be a little hard to stop. This is fine if we have the time, energy, and other resources to spend on it without hurting the other corners of our lives.

Most parents don't. We have other claims on our time. Start with setting up PACE plans for communications and gathering together during emergencies. If you have those in place, many of the other factors become easier. Additional levels of preparation can be important but can also wait.

88 Have Two Major Plans

Think about your safety training at work: that big three-ring binder with a page for every conceivable emergency and small but meaningful differences between what to do in a hurricane versus what to do in a tornado.

That book is great for lawyers and insurance executives, but for families trying to stay safe, it's nonsense. On the spot, with the stress of a crisis, could you remember the details? Could your kids?

Simplicity is a necessity for family emergency plans, and that starts with simplifying which plans to use in different situations.

In my estimation, families need two plans for home emergencies: a bug-in plan, and a bug-out plan

Bug-In Plans. Your family bug-in plan covers every emergency where the right move is to stay at home to shelter in place. In all cases, from a home invasion to a city-wide blackout, the plan covers the same steps.

Somebody decides on and announces the bug-in. Everybody runs to the safe room or other designated meeting place. You stay there until the situation is over, it turns into a bug-out situation, or you decide in a long-term emergency that it's safe to move around the house.

When you build yours, answer the following questions:

- Who decides when to activate the bug-in plan?
- How do they communicate this to family members?
- Are there family members who can't physically bug in on their own, and what will you do about them?
- Where does everybody meet during a bug-in situation?
- How will you prepare that room?
- What immediate supplies do you need for a bug-in situation?
- How will you communicate with the outside?
- What role does each family member play during a bug-in?
- What will you do if a family member is too far away to bug in with you?
- Who decides when the bug-in is over and how do they decide?

With this as the foundation, you can build a solid bug-in plan that helps your family manage most appropriate emergencies.

Bug-Out Plans. A bug-out plan covers all emergencies where you need to get out of the house, or even the area. A house fire or approaching tornado both call for a bug-out. So might a home invasion. As with bug-in plans, your bug-out plan applies the same early response to all situations.

Somebody (or an alarm) announces the bug-out. Everybody grabs any needed gear and exits the house through a designated route. You all meet at a rendezvous point you agreed on ahead of time, then decide what to do next.

When you build yours, answer the following questions:

- Who and what decides when to activate the bug-out plan?
- How do they communicate this to family members?

- Are there family members who can't physically bug out on their own, and what will you do about them?
- Are the escape routes from your home reliably open and free of obstacles?
- What clothes, gear, or equipment should each person get and take with them?
- Who is responsible to make sure others get out of the house safely?
- Where will everybody meet once you leave the house?
- What is the next step after everybody meets at the appointed place?

For families with older children, you can have two bug-out plans. One has everybody meet outside the house or across the street, as would be appropriate in a fire or home invasion. The other has everybody meet at the car so you can leave the area, like you would with an incoming natural disaster.

Families with younger children should have all bug-out plans meet outside the home. You can go from there to the car, and that way the littlest ones only have to remember one plan.

89 Build a Simple Safe Room

It might feel like instructions on safe rooms would be more appropriate in the Crime Prevention section than the Emergency Prep section, but here's the thing.

A safe room is a secure area for the family to gather when there's danger, stocked with things you'll need in an emergency. The focus is on that emergency being a criminal invading your home, but there's no reason you can't use it for any bug-in situation.

Even if you don't have to huddle in the room for the duration of the emergency, getting together in the safe room is a good first step. You can do a head count, access your most important supplies, then move forward from a place of security and reassurance.

Where to Put Your Safe Room. This is the first question to ask when considering your safe room. It must be a place with a door that locks, that can fit all members of your household without stress or pain.

Many families designate the parents' bedroom as the safe room. This makes sense on the surface. It's where the safest adults are. It (usually) has a locking door. If your family keeps guns, they're probably in there.

If your bedroom is the safe room, the more vulnerable members of the family must come to you. If some are less mobile, like an infant or an elder, you must leave your safe room and lead them back to it. Going to fetch them in the middle of an emergency drastically increases how much time your family is at risk.

Instead, make your safe room in the bedroom of the least mobile member of your family. When an emergency hits where you need a safe room, they don't need to go anywhere. Everybody gathers to them.

Area Denial. Once you've decided what room the whole family will gather in during an emergency, the next step is to think about how to keep bad guys out.

This is where some of our minds go to five-and-six figure home projects that lock the room down like a Swiss vault. There's no need for that. Instead, see to three things.

- Secure the door. Replace the flimsy, hollow-core door to most interior rooms with solid wood. This is less expensive than you're probably imagining and helps with fire safety, too.

- Install a good lock, one with both a door latch and a deadbolt. For the strike plate, replace the screws that came in the package with three-inch screws to maximize security.
- Make a barricade available. A heavy bookcase, movable bed, chest of drawers, or changing station can all be dragged in front of the door to make it harder to force. If possible, identify a series of items you can stack all the way to the opposite wall.

With those in place, you can deny safe room access to all but the most determined of invaders.

If your safe room is the bedroom of a toddler, child, or elder, secure furniture to the wall to prevent tipping. Since you might need to tip the furniture to make a barricade, keep a tool in the room to help you do that. A demolition bar or claw hammer should be all you need…just make sure it's up and out of reach for smaller children.

Stocking Up. You might be in your safe room for a while. At a minimum, your safe room should include the following:

- A bottle of water for each member of your family
- A long-lasting snack (like granola bars) for each member of your family
- A flashlight with extra batteries
- A land line phone, prepaid cell phone, or at least a charger and cable
- A copy of your family's 911 script, for young ones to read if necessary
- A basic first-aid kit

Some things many families opt to also include:

- Whatever self-defense weapon you are comfortable keeping and using
- A set of house keys to throw out the window when the police arrive
- Longer-term emergency supplies. You have to keep them somewhere
- A solution for needing to go to the bathroom
- Emergency medication family members need, like an epi pen or asthma inhaler
- A pocket knife or multitool

Assemble the safe room kit, then check and restock it just like you do your other emergency packs.

If you are using a child's room, use common sense and caution about securing potentially dangerous supplies. A locking tackle box or combination safe works well for this purpose.

90 Stock a Full First-Aid Kit

Boo-boos and minor injuries are part of growing up and one of the ways children learn how to assess and manage risk. That means we, as parents, should fully stock a first-aid kit so we can fix those boo-boos as they happen.

You can build your own kit for less than $100. Your kit will consist of four kinds of first aid supplies:

- Boo-boo kit
- Trauma supplies
- Durable equipment
- Medications

Although each family's needs are different, here I'll go over the important elements of each kind of supply.

Boo-Boo Kit. The boo-boo kit contains things you'll need to handle the scrapes, scratches, nicks, cuts, bruises, and goose eggs that come with a childhood lived well. These include:

- Band-Aids in two or three different sizes
- Gauze pads in 3"x3" and 4"x4"
- Sterile wipes in individual packets
- Antibiotic cream
- Cotton swabs
- Bee sting wipes or stick
- Paper medical tape
- A bag of frozen peas (kept in the freezer)

Trauma Supplies. Sometimes somebody gets hurt badly enough that they need professional medical attention. At those times, you need the right gear to provide care until professionals arrive.

- Trauma pads or maxi pads
- Cloth medical tape
- Self-sticking medical wrap
- Eye bandages
- Eye wash
- SAM splint
- Israeli bandage or tourniquet kit

If you're not sure what some of these items are, do a quick Google search. You can also find a full description in my blog or on my YouTube channel. Look for the interview with set medic Steve Mullins, Season One Episode Ten.

Durable Equipment. The supplies listed so far are one-use, or run out eventually. You will also want some gear that lasts. A well-stocked family first-aid kit should have at least:

- Thermometer (and baby thermometer for wee ones)
- Flashlight
- Permanent marker
- Tweezers
- Safety pins
- Triangle bandage
- Space blanket
- Medical scissors

Medications. A first-aid kit is incomplete without your medicine cabinet. At a minimum, you should have:

- Pain and fever relief like ibuprofen, acetaminophen, or aspirin
- Stomach relief like Pepto-Bismol
- Allergy relief like Sudafed or Benadryl
- Baby aspirin, if anybody in the family (or regular visitors) has a heart condition
- Daytime and nighttime cold and flu relief

One More: Personal Items. Every family has special needs and personal preferences that will add to their kit.

For example, we are a family of athletes with seasonal allergies, so our kit includes Tiger Balm, Benadryl, Claritin, Sudafed, and cortisone cream.

Any family with a member with a food allergy will want some prescription-strength antihistamines and an epi pen. Families with smaller kids need child versions of the medications I listed above.

You'll also want regular prescription medications anybody in the family needs. I recommend getting one extra batch of each to keep in the first-aid kit, so you're not in trouble if something interrupts your refills.

Where to Buy It. Most items on this list you can get from Amazon for less than you'll pay at your local drug store or big-box store. The Band-Aids, gauze, medical tape, and tweezers you can get from your local dollar store at surprisingly good quality.

If you band together with some friends, neighbors, or family, you can get even better prices by ordering in bulk from medical supply wholesalers.

Where to Store It. Storing your family first-aid kit means answering two questions: What kind of container should you use, and where should it live in the house?

For the container, tool bags, toolboxes, and tackle boxes work well. I use one of those plastic fastener boxes with transparent drawers. Ten minutes with a label maker, and it's stocked and easy to navigate.

Where to keep your first-aid kit in your home requires finding a balance. A first-aid kit should be easy to spot and access, but also young children should not be able to access any potentially dangerous supplies.

Only you know your house well enough to decide how to strike that balance.

Emergency Preparedness Action Plan

General advice doesn't do much good, especially for people with free time as limited as active parents. Here's a quick checklist of the most vital action items you can start with today about being ready for emergencies.

Do these this week and you're on your way to a safer family:

- ❏ Create a family communication chat on Facebook, and make sure everybody knows to check there in emergencies.
- ❏ Inventory your home first aid kit…
- ❏ …and order supplies to fill it up.

Find an hour soon and take action to become even safer:

- ❏ Install a simple lock on the door to whatever room you designate as your family's safe room.
- ❏ Stock your safe room with snacks and water.
- ❏ Build a basic underbed bag for each bedroom in the house.

Make time for these important long-term projects to become the safest family on your block:

- ❏ Set up your family's emergency communications tree, updating any phone numbers as necessary.
- ❏ For the next month, buy an extra can of food and a flat of bottled water for each family member when you go on your weekly shopping trip.
- ❏ Build and write out your family's basic emergency plan.

CRIME PREVENTION

Introduction by Randy King

Randy King is an internationally recognized self-defense educator and conflict communication specialist with over fifteen years of experience in personal protection and safety training. Known for his practical, no-nonsense approach, Randy has delivered seminars and workshops across North America and Europe. As the author of Before, During, After: The Timeline of Self-Defense *and host of the accompanying podcast, Randy simplifies complex safety concepts into actionable steps for everyday people.*

As a lifelong student and teacher of self-defense, I've seen the pivotal role awareness and preparation play in preventing harm. Whether training individuals to navigate dangerous encounters or creating proactive safety plans, one truth remains constant: small, intentional actions can drastically improve personal safety.

Crime prevention isn't about living in fear or constructing a fortress around your family. It's about cultivating habits and environments that make you and your loved ones less appealing to those who wish harm. The good news? This doesn't require superhuman skills or endless time. It's about knowing your options, understanding common risks, and implementing practical solutions.

In this chapter, you'll find a toolkit of strategies, many of which are simple, low cost, or even free. From recognizing and avoiding transitional spaces to installing DIY home security upgrades, these tips empower you and your family to feel safe, not scared. The goal isn't just to avoid bad outcomes but to build confidence and competence that radiates from every member of your household. After all, a family that works together on safety grows closer in trust and resilience.

Take these tools seriously, but remember to enjoy the learning process. Preparing isn't just a duty; it can be a rewarding and fun journey toward living a safer, happier life.

91 Learn One or Two Moves

I've trained in martial arts since I was eleven years old. That's (mumble mumble) years. I love learning new and exciting moves with escalating degrees of complexity.

To protect myself, though, I don't need to do that. Neither do you. Here's why.

Analysis Paralysis. The art I have my highest rank in is kenpo karate. In kenpo, we're taught to respond to attack X with move A, and to attack Z with move B, and so on.

As you advance, you end up having moves A1, A2, A3, and more for each attack X. That's part of the fun.

When you're attacked you have a split second to react. When you know an encyclopedia of potential responses, a lot can go wrong.

- If you know three ways to respond to an incoming right-hand punch, you might still be deciding between them when the punch hits your nose.
- If you know different responses to a right punch, a right push, and a right knife attack, you could lose precious time trying to figure out which one is coming toward you.
- The decisions could lead to freezing instead of fight or flight, because those higher-order thinking skills go out the window when things get dicey.

As much as I love kenpo and similar technique-based systems, I consider 99 percent of the individual techniques I've learned purely recreational.

The OODA Loop. One reason for this is what the tacticool crowd calls the OODA loop. It was initially taught to fighter pilots but maps well enough to personal defense or any high-stress situation that evolves (or devolves) rapidly.

OODA stands for Observe, Orient, Decide, Act. It follows the natural process of responding to any stimulus. You Observe something. You Orient by assessing what it means. You Decide what to do about it. You Act on that decision. Then you Observe what happens next. Simple and intuitive.

But there's a catch. If something interrupts the flow, for example, a punch to your face while you're deciding whether to use an outward block or an inward bracing block, it starts the whole process over. You end up stuck in an OODOODOODOOD loop instead of the OODA that can save your life.

One Size Fits Most. Overwhelmingly, the first attacks on people follow the same basic patterns. They're almost always:

- A right hand
- Sometimes empty, sometimes with a weapon
- Aimed at the head
- If possible from ambush or from surprise

For women, a wrist grab is a close second, but half the time or more that right-hand attack is following close behind.

Knowing this, we can protect ourselves from the most likely attacks with a single move that:

- Protects the front and left side of our head
- Works for empty hands and armed attackers
- Can protect from odd angles if we turn around
- Also defends against a wrist grab

A lot of simple motions do this. You can look some up on You-Tube, or check out Tony Blauer's SPEAR system, Rory Miller's Dracula's Cape, or the video on my channel about the "Oh Crap! Block."

Having that move down cold (see below) gives you something to do immediately if an attacker ever comes at you. From that initial response, you can follow up with other actions. It might be shoving the attacker and running away. It might be a double-leg takedown from your high school wrestling days. It might be going for the eyes. Whatever works for you and the situation.

Drill to Reflex. A little bit of bad news. You still have to train. Not as much as I do, but more than not training at all. This one-move strategy only works if you have drilled until it's what you *automatically* do if attacked.

Don't worry. That comes quicker than you're imagining.

92 Play Awareness Games

Here's the difference between the mind-set of a martial artist who was bullied as a child versus a compassionate woman who wasn't.

My wife and I were in London, on a long tube ride. I tried to show off my long-held, hard-earned tactical acumen by telling her an awareness game I play in situations like this. It doesn't have a name, at least I don't know one, but consists of scanning any crowd I'm in and identifying four people:

- The person most likely to be a problem
- The person most likely to cause a problem (not always the same person as above)
- The person I would ask for help first
- The most dangerous person in the crowd

Upon hearing my description, and my analysis of the car we were in, she said, "Oh yeah! You're playing the zombie game!"

Then she told me about the game she plays in crowds, where she identifies the people she would team up with in the zombie apocalypse. She didn't have a list, but she'd look at each person and base her decision on their likely demeanor, skill set, and level of preparedness.

Like I said, her mind-set was very different, but both games share a central idea.

Awareness Games Make Us Safer. Playing that kind of game in a crowd makes us aware of the people around us. Mine was based on identifying specific threats so I could be prepared if they became a problem. Hers was based on finding resources and collaborators.

Both meant scanning every individual in the crowd and making an assessment. At the macro level, that's excellent situational awareness. We know from experience, anecdote, and research that awareness deters criminals.

At a deeper level, those initial thoughts lead to creating a plan. If I identify the person in a crowd most likely to be a problem, I can hardly help running through some scenarios about how I would deal with them. My wife's plan for a zombie apocalypse won't actually come up, but if she needed somebody to call an ambulance, she would have already picked the best candidate.

It doesn't matter which of those games you play, or if you play another game altogether. Any sort of awareness game will improve your ability to defend yourself, send a message to potential predators watching you, and teach your children how to live safer lives.

Scenario Planning. This touches on the most important self-defense benefit of martial arts training. Time spent on the mat includes endless hours of learning and rehearsing specific responses to being attacked. If a bad guy throws a punch at you,

you've trained to respond with a set series of motions. You don't have to decide what to do on the spot, which is a bad time to make decisions.

If you play awareness games, it naturally leads to scenario planning. You come up with ideas about how to handle different kinds of people, what to do in various safety situations, and who you would ask for help if you were attacked.

93 When in Doubt, Draft

Not too long ago, my wife and I were going to a concert in downtown Portland. We ended up parking about eight blocks away and walking in. It was not a savory neighborhood, but it was early evening and we're both pretty savvy. I was confident we would be safe.

About two blocks in, I noticed we were being followed by a professional woman in her late twenties. She caught up to maybe three paces behind us, then stayed there. She didn't talk to, or even acknowledge us, but to a stranger watching she looked like she was part of our group.

She was drafting while walking alone in a sketchy neighborhood.

This had never occurred to me before, so I asked Beverly Baker, one of the smartest people working in women's safety today. Her response was, "Oh, yeah. Women do that all the time."

This is, apparently, a thing.

Most women reading this book are probably nodding their heads right now. The rest of us can start applying it today.

What Is Drafting? In sports, athletes draft to reduce air and water resistance during a race. When a runner moves forward, they leave a lower-pressure zone in their wake because their motion parts the air. That pocket of lower resistance requires less energy to move through.

It's a tiny amount of less energy, not enough to help you or me with a local 5k fun run…but for professional-level racers, it can make a meaningful difference.

For safety, it's about creating a pocket of *greater* perceived resistance. Criminals dislike risk. The more people in a group, the riskier it is to victimize them. By staying near a larger group, we can give the illusion of being a bigger risk than we really are.

How to Draft. If you're a woman by herself, or anybody walking with children, drafting is simple. You don't have to worry about scaring or offending the group you're drafting from. That woman before the concert, for example, didn't worry me. I'm an athletic male martial artist and was walking with my very street-savvy, urban-raised wife. For that woman, the process was simple:

- Step One: Identify a group that seems safe to draft off of.
- Step Two: Walk faster until you're two or three paces behind.
- Step Three: Stay there for as long as you need.

Step One is the trickiest part, but we can pair it with the predator profiling mentioned later in this section. A woman walking alone was safe to choose a middle-aged man and his vastly more attractive and intelligent wife. She'd be fine with a group of women, or with a family. She might not want to try her luck with a half-dozen drunk men in their twenties.

For men without our children, we also have to consider how our drafting might impact the people we follow. If we tried to draft off of a woman or small group of women, we might leave them feeling unsafe. We're better off joining that group of drunk twentysomethings.

Standing Still. One challenge with drafting is what to do while choosing who we want to draft behind. Criminals target people who seem hesitant or disoriented. Standing on the street watching people pass can leave you looking like an attractive target. At the same time, walking alone into the street before you find a suitable draft partner can also be dangerous.

If you can manage it, watch from indoors through a window. Find your draft partner, then walk outside as they pass by the door. If that's not an option, stand somewhere natural and look attentive, like you're waiting for somebody. Consider nodding to yourself, or even waving, when you see who you want to walk with.

94 Install Lights and Cameras

There's a lot of advice out there about keeping your home unfriendly to bad guys. Of that advice, installing lights and cameras has the most support from police, reformed criminals, and data collection professionals like insurance companies and security firms.

There are many good reasons that's true. Both deter criminals of all stripes by increasing their chances of getting caught during and after a crime

John Riddle, a retired police officer who spent years investigating burglaries, reports that often, if a criminal sees a camera, he stares straight at it, as if saying to himself, "Hey, is that a camera?" thus thoughtfully providing a full front facial image for police to use later.

Installing or upgrading your home lighting and cameras might be the best safety move you make this year.

Lights. Lights deter criminals by making it harder for them to hide. To install lights on your own property, walk around at night. Note the places too dark to see a cat, and you'll know where you need to add illumination.

Motion sensor lights are the best option here. They don't waste electricity when you don't need them, and they respond to movement. This can give the illusion that somebody is home and awake.

Solar-powered motion sensor lights are reliable in most climates and available online or at your local big box hardware store for under $40. Models with a battery backup cost about the same.

Camera. Cameras deter crime by increasing the risk of coming on your property and can help police identify criminals afterward. They can also give you a sense of what happens on your street if you review the footage from time to time.

If you only install one camera, put it at your doorway. This records everybody who approaches or enters through the door, which is helpful for crime prevention, tracking deliveries, and checking who's at the door before you open it.

If you want more cameras, consider the following locations: all other exterior doors, your driveway (especially if you park outside), walkways, the corners of your house, and positioned to view gates in your fence.

Interior cameras can also improve safety, but not everybody is comfortable with that amount of surveillance in their private spaces.

Wireless, internet-based cameras are available for under $50 per unit from multiple sources online. They're cheap, easy to install, and connect with your phone.

The disadvantage is that they are only as secure as the Wi-Fi network you connect them to. If somebody can access your network, they can access all the footage or disconnect the cameras prior to approaching your home.

On the other hand, wired cameras require professional installation. They are more expensive and don't usually integrate as well with your other home devices.

My recommendation: get the wireless option. Set up a separate network for your Internet of Things devices, including your cameras. Create a secure password and share it with nobody.

Action. Your cameras, and to a lesser extent your lights, do less good if you never use them. Modern internet cameras text you when they pick up motion, but after a hundred false alarms we fall out of the habit of checking.

This is one of those trade-offs between safety and convenience. With my system, I respond to alerts late at night and check daytime footage during idle time to keep an eye on the neighborhood.

One Last Little Thing. With the solar lights and wireless cameras, you will spend some time up on a ladder installing them. Practice good ladder safety. Set it on level, stable ground. Have an assistant hold it steady and hand you items. Keep below the upper rungs and don't stretch to reach things.

If you fall off a ladder while installing family safety equipment, the injuries won't kill you, but the irony might.

95 Be Alert in Transitional Spaces

There's a concept called "liminal spaces." These are places where people don't really go to. They move *through* them while going from one space to another. Airports, bus stations, and city streets are liminal spaces. So are the hallways in schools and office buildings.

If you've been in a mostly empty liminal space, you've felt that wrongness. There's a creepy factor to them, because they're different than our minds expect them to be.

Transitional spaces are the equivalent when we talk about crime prevention instead of aesthetics. These are where people move from one place to another, or from one state to another. Some are also liminal spaces. Others aren't.

Criminals often gather in transitional spaces, looking for victims.

What's So Dangerous? Transitional spaces pose a lot of advantages for people who want to do harm. They:

- Have lots of traffic, offering a variety of potential victims
- Grant quick and easy escape after the crime
- Tend to be lightly staffed and poorly secured
- Are noisy and full of visual stimuli. Crime can go unobserved.
- Often include people waiting for something. A loitering criminal won't be noticed.
- Sometimes contain people carrying more valuables than usual—for example, leaving a mall after shopping or carrying a laptop to work.
- Rapidly empty and refill. Nobody stays long enough to notice suspicious behavior.

Transitional spaces are also transitional in our minds. Think about the last few times you walked from a shop to your car. How many of those times were you focused on what was going on in that space, compared to how many times you were thinking about what just happened or the next errand on your list?

That's human nature. Transitional spaces are for moving through, so our minds tend to move through them just like our bodies. That inattention gives criminals an opportunity that's less common in other places.

Common Transitional Spaces. By the time you've reached this sentence you've probably already thought of a few transitional spaces you move through often. The most common transitional spaces include:

- Parking lots and garages
- Bus stops and stations
- Park walkways and jogging paths
- Some city streets
- Portions of city parks
- Elevators

Airports, bus stations, and train stations are also common transitional spaces, but they're not high-risk spots for violent crime. They are more highly staffed and secured, and people tend to move through them in groups.

What to Do About Them. If you've made it this far in the book, you can likely predict what I'm about to say. Deal safely with transitional spaces by slowing down and paying attention.

As you pass into a transitional space, pause and take a breath. Scan the area to your immediate left and right, then look ahead at the path to your destination. Look for people acting strangely, gathering in groups, or who otherwise catch your attention. For each person who does, ask yourself why. If anything seems off, go back inside. Get a staff member to escort you, wait for the suspicious people to leave, or call a friend to come help. If all else fails, wait for another person to exit and draft off of them as far as you can.

Once you move into the transitional space, stay focused on what's happening. Continue to scan your surroundings. Check behind you, and where you're going, for signs of trouble. Focus on your pace and demeanor so you give off a competent, confident vibe.

96 Learn Your Predator Profile

In self-defense, we spend a lot of time thinking about how we act, how we think, and what we observe.

That's good, but at the same time we don't often think what's going on in the bad guys' minds.

If we understand what the bad guys who might target us want, and what they're afraid of, it can help us prevent violent crime before it starts.

What Do the Bad Guys Want? At the most basic, there are two kinds of bad guys. Resource predators want your stuff. Process predators want you. Some resource predators just want whatever they can sell. Others specifically want cell phones, or laptops, or cash, or jewelry. Some process predators want a small victim who's easy to cow and intimidate. Others want to make a trophy of somebody who looks intimidating.

Most predators are good at what they do, which means they've identified the kind of person most likely to have what they want. They have a type. For example:

- A smash-and-run mugger who just wants easy money is likely to target women and small men wearing nice clothes.
- A woman who wants to steal money might target men who look like they're in town on business.
- A group of young men out to feel tough might target other young men in numbers smaller than their own.

Step One in setting up your own safety profile is understanding what kinds of bad guys might consider you a target.

I'm a large, male, aging jock who moves like he's trained for a long time. I wear no jewelry and don't spend much on clothes. That keeps many kinds of criminal away from me. Mostly, I need to worry about three kinds of bad guys.

- Aggressive panhandlers might approach me in front of my wife and kids because they think I won't want to look cheap in front of them.
- Women running a scam might focus on the *aging* jock part, trying to trick me into letting down my guard by suggesting, "The old man's still got it."
- Some process predators looking to feel tough might also zero in on the aging part, thinking they could take the middle-aged guy and win points because I look like I'm still in shape.

On the other hand, I don't usually need to worry about muggers. It's also unlikely anybody's going to roofie me at a party. Nobody's going to pull up in a van, grab me off the road, and sell me into sex trafficking. I don't need to worry about those threats.

What Are Bad Guys Afraid Of? Bad guys are afraid of getting caught and getting hurt. The trick is to make sure you present in a way that emphasizes those fears. Some universal ways to do this include:

- Staying visibly alert by looking around at eye level
- Moving with confidence: arms swinging, medium gait
- Not looking at our phones while out and about
- Staying sober and off drugs in public
- Keeping in shape

Beyond that, you can look at your list of personal predators and make some strong predictions about specific things they might be afraid of.

That aggressive panhandler fears little, because it would be illegal for me to attack him, but he knows he can't spend too much time on any one person. That drunk-rolling woman likely fears physical attacks and the police. The process predator who wants the fight fears being made to look or feel weak and foolish. Each of these fears presents a potential strategy for avoiding their notice or escaping them if they begin to make contact.

Take some time. Do some research. Ask some experts. Answer these questions for each member of your family. You can make this as formal or informal as you like, but this kind of preparatory work can help your family feel safer, and be safer, for the rest of your lives.

97 Case Your Home

One decision I made early on when creating *Safest Family on the Block* was to not cover fraud, identity theft, and property crimes. Your family's lives are far more important than your money, and I want to focus on physical safety.

But burglary is another matter. Burglars target your stuff, not your family, but if they show up when you're home, that can quickly escalate into violence.

One of the simplest and best things you can do to prevent burglaries is to case your home.

Look at your home from the outside from the point of view of a burglar. If you were looking for a house to steal things from, would you want to steal things from this house? What signs and signals does your house and property send that might invite bad guys in or tell them to seek crime elsewhere?

What Do Burglars Look For? According to many of the crime prevention experts I spoke with, burglars and most other criminals care about if there's something worth stealing inside your home and whether or not somebody will see them stealing it.

With that in mind, look for factors that make your home a harder-looking target. What might tell a criminal your home will be hard to enter? Or signal there's little of value to steal? What suggests they're likely to get caught?

Likewise, what indicates there's valuable loot inside that's easy to access and get away with?

Start with driving slowly past your house, then walk past it. Do this twice: once in daylight, once after dark. Homes look very different in those two conditions. Burglars usually enter homes in the afternoon, but they case homes during both times. You should as well.

Here's what to look for.

Likelihood of Success. A burglar looks for houses with stuff that's easy and worthwhile to steal. As you case your home, look for things like:

- Windows without curtains or blinds, showing electronics or other high-end goods to anybody looking in
- Tools and sports equipment in the garage or shed
- Boxes from expensive items in your trash or recycling
- Clear signs of wealth in your yard, on your porch, or on visible exterior walls
- Frequent delivery packages
- Personalized license plates, high-end cars, or other prestige vehicles in the driveway
- High-end landscaping that shows you have lots of disposable income
- Bumper stickers, or posters inside, that show you travel frequently

These are just a few examples of a home a criminal might consider worth the risk of entering. Make a note of each, then get busy making sure they're not visible from the outside. I'm not saying you shouldn't have nice things you enjoy. I'm saying those things are nobody's business but yours.

Likelihood of Getting Caught. No matter how much loot a burglar can grab, it does them no good if they get caught. For this, you'll look for security factors like:

- Does your front yard have a high privacy fence, bushy plants, or other things to hide behind while approaching your home?
- Are the gates to your backyard always closed and latched?
- Do windows look easy to access?
- Is your garage door frequently left open?
- Is it easy to predict when people will or won't be home?
- Do you have adequate lighting in the front, side, and back yards?
- Are cameras up, working, and visible?
- Are there signs of a dog or children on the property?
- Do you have indications of an alarm system or security company?
- Is it easy to walk silently while approaching your home?
- Is your yard poorly maintained, suggesting security will be equally slipshod?

Look for signs a burglar can get in and out easily and unobserved versus signs that you take informed steps toward crime prevention.

98 Upgrade Home Security with Simple DIY

Homes are pretty well-designed tools for keeping us warm and dry and letting us sleep safe from dangers that go bump in the night. They're not perfect, though. Which is why it's good that we can upgrade that safety easily and inexpensively even if we're not particularly handy. Here are four of my favorites.

Cut Down Some Dowels. Your standard window or sliding patio door is embarrassingly easy to jimmy open if it's only defended by its manufacturer's lock. Fix this by cutting down dowels and jamming them closed.

Measure the trough of your closed window, at the bottom. Buy a ½-inch diameter dowel (1-inch diameter for glass sliders). Cut the dowel down to ¼ inch shorter than the width of your trough. The difference is so there's not trouble if the wood swells with humidity or heat. Once it's cut, drop it into the trough of your window. It's easy to remove when you want to open it and does the same work as a deadbolt when you want it closed.

This only works for windows that open horizontally. For vertically opening windows, you can buy specialized equipment that does the same thing. If you're feeling ambitious, though, use the same method and add a two-dollar clip to the window to hold it in place.

Put Down Gravel. It's pretty easy to walk quietly on grass, concrete, and paving stones, but not even cats can walk quietly on gravel. Call your local landscaping company and order a yard or so worth of gravel, then use it to cover key walkways on your property.

The best ones for this are the ones leading along the side of your house, from the front to the backyard. If you can only do some walkways, those are the ones. If you can do all your walkways, so much the better. It only takes a layer an inch deep for it to do what you want it to do.

Replace Your Door Screws. Open your door and look at the lock. There's a piece of metal on the door jamb called a strike plate. It's one of the things that makes it harder for somebody to kick the metal of the lock through the thin wood of the door's frame. It's in there with two screws.

Thing is, those screws are usually ½ inch or ¾ inch deep. That's not enough to stop a forceful hit to the door. Get a pair of 3-inch wood screws. Pull out the short ones that came with the lock. Replace them with those. For a dollar in materials and ten minutes of your time, you've exponentially increased the security of your front door's lock.

Now go do it for the rest of your exterior doors, and for any locking interior doors you want to harden against intruders.

Trim the Bushes. One thing bad guys look for when deciding what houses to target is how visible they will be from inside and outside. A house with thick hedges and bushy trees in the yard offers places to hide while entering and leaving. Foliage that blocks the windows means they can be inside unobserved from the street.

Take an afternoon, some loppers, and a hedge trimmer to fix this once a year. With those hiding places trimmed back, criminals know there's nowhere to hide...and smart criminals know you're paying attention to security.

If you have a two-story house, keep an eye on tree limbs. If any grow long and thick enough to offer access to upper-floor windows, trim those branches back.

99 Should You Buy a Gun?

I get asked a version of this question more often than any other when meeting with clients worried about violent crime.

It's tricky, politicized, and personal. For some people, guns are only a source of fear and worry. For others, guns are part of their personal and cultural identity. Many millions of people fall in between.

Every family and situation is different. I can't give a universal yes or no answer, but I can bring up some points for you to consider.

Default to No. A gun in your home makes your home more dangerous. Just like having a table saw, a swimming pool, a medicine cabinet, or a riding lawnmower.

Ideally, it makes your home more dangerous for people who mean your family harm…but on the far more frequent days when none of those are available, the risk is real.

That's why I say default to no. If you're on the fence about it, that added danger should break the tie.

How Willing Are You to Train? Think for a minute about the last time you tried to take a photo with some kind of time pressure. Was it smooth and easy, or did you fumble? How good was the photo, compared to ones you took when you had plenty of time?

You use your phone's camera far more often than you are likely to practice with a gun…and the situation will be infinitely more stressful than rushing to take a picture.

For a gun to be a good idea, you must train hard—both range time and drawing swiftly. If you have the time and the willingness to spend multiple hours each month training, then a gun can be a valuable tool. But only if you can and will do that.

What Is Your Storage Solution? Raising children to respect guns is important, but kids sometimes do dumb things. Every month there's a tragic story about children playing with guns, even kids who knew better.

Also, your kids aren't the only people you need to worry about accessing your guns. Department of Justice statistics show just under four hundred thousand guns are stolen each year.

It's worth it to spend a few extra dollars to get personalized training from somebody who knows you, your family, and your home. Use it to design a safe storage solution that's in place before a firearm enters your family.

Ancillary Knowledge. If you decide you do want to have a gun in your home for self-protection, a related set of skills will help you mitigate the risks and dangers associated with keeping a gun in the house.

- **Trauma medicine**. A house with a gun in it needs adults who know how to treat a gunshot wound.
- **Self-defense law in your area**. These vary widely, and may or may not match your personal ethics or what you already think is true.
- **Firearm carry law in your area**. These are much more complicated than many people expect, with heavy penalties for mistakes.
- **Mental health history** of everybody likely to be in your home. A history of depression, anxiety, suicidal ideation, or similar diagnoses can increase how dangerous a gun in your home might be.
- **Architecture in your home**, to the level that you know which doors and walls will stop a bullet from your gun, and which won't. The home defense plan you build and practice should be based on this information.

Without this knowledge, and the equipment you need to apply it, a gun in your home becomes exponentially more dangerous.

Bottom Line. I'm not saying don't arm yourself against the bad guys. I truly believe most of us should. But arming ourselves takes much more than just owning a weapon.

100   Confidence Reduces Victimhood

I mentioned this earlier in the book, but it's important enough to merit some more detail. That 1981 study by Grayson and Stein is a guide to greatly reducing the chances a predator will choose you as a victim.

This is true whether the predator is a mugger, a serial killer, or a con artist. It's true for your kids whether the predator is a bully or a coach grooming them.

I mentioned Grayson and Stein's study back in the Golden Rules chapter. They asked criminals to identify likely targets by watching video of a busy intersection.

Between interviews with the criminals and their own observations, they learned the key factor was the appearance of confidence.

People who move with confidence deter criminal attacks because that appearance suggests they will be harder to victimize. People who seem underconfident attract predators because they are more likely to go along with what people tell them.

How to Show Confidence? By studying the videos, Grayson and Stein identified several common traits in the body language of people the criminals rated as too tough to attack:

- Head up while walking
- Eyes forward and alert
- Straight but relaxed posture
- Shoulders back
- Symmetry in movement
- Medium to long stride
- Decisive movements

You can picture in your head what this looks like out in the world, maybe with somebody in mind. Whether or not this is your natural way of walking and moving, it can be worth it to practice this until it becomes natural...and to teach our kids to move the same way.

"But wait! There's more!" Study after study have also shown that posture can impact mood. You've probably experienced that yourself, getting an unexpected boost of energy when you stood up from a hunched posture.

This means that if you move like you have confidence, it will actually build your confidence. You won't just show that you're not an easy victim. You will actually become a hard target.

The Long Game. Moving with confidence doesn't just deter street crime in the moment. Predators who work over longer periods also avoid confident people.

A long con artist will approach somebody who looks easy to lead and control. So will a serial abuser when they choose their next relationship-slash-victim. Bullies at school pick people they can intimidate and demean. Child sex predators choose victims with low confidence.

Confidence or its lack isn't the only factor in how criminals choose victims, but it is one of the most important. It's also something we can control starting today.

See Also: Phones. The Greyson and Stein study happened a quarter century before cell phones became pervasive. Were they to conduct their research today, I am certain that "Not staring at their cell phone" would be on the top of their list of traits that made harder targets.

Crime Prevention Action Plan

General advice doesn't do much good, especially for people with free time as limited as active parents. Here's a quick checklist of the most vital action items you can start with today about dealing with crime.

Do these this week and you're on your way to a safer family:

- ❏ Spend five minutes identifying the transitional spaces you move through most often during your normal routine.
- ❏ Walk by your house during the day to see how inviting it is for burglars or home invasion…
- ❏ …and again at night.

Find an hour soon and take action to become even safer:

- ❏ Play an awareness game with your family the next time you all go out.
- ❏ Practice "drafting" the next time you're walking in an urban space.
- ❏ Scroll your social media to see how much information you are giving about what's inside your home and when people are likely to be there.

Make time for these important long-term projects to become the safest family on your block:

- ❏ Buy and install lights and cameras for your home. If you already have them, fill in any gaps in your coverage.
- ❏ Take a basic self-defense course, keeping an eye out for the single self-defense move that would work best as your default.
- ❏ Talk with your co-parent about your personal predator profiles, and how you can best deter the most likely attackers.

THE 101ˢᵀ HABIT

101 Practice What You Teach

I have an uncle, George. He spent the first thirty or so years of his adult life in Marine Corps Special Forces, beginning with time in Vietnam. He spent the second half as a school administrator.

His viewpoint on safety, especially child safety, is unique and well-earned. He shares much of that viewpoint in an interview for my show, and I encourage you to watch the whole thing. During that interview, he shared with me once one of the most important safety facts I've ever heard.

A plan you don't rehearse is not a plan. It's a wish.

You can come up with the best plan in the world, sitting with your family at the table in a well-lit room with a full belly and a happy face. I recommend you do exactly that.

But if all you do is make the plan and hope everybody remembers it when things get serious, you are in for a rough time.

When emergencies strike, we get hit with a lot of hormones and other body chemicals that increase our individual ability to survive serious injuries. That's good if we're being attacked by a saber-tooth tiger, but not great when we need to manage complex safety solutions in the modern world.

Under that level of stress, we lose higher-order thinking skills. Our senses and motor function begin to deteriorate. Our ability to come up with and carry out a good plan goes right out the window.

So does most of our ability to remember a plan we came up with one evening months or years ago.

That's why the 101st habit is to practice the habits listed in this book. Some are motor skills you just have to do often enough to internalize. Some are routines to make part of your calendar. Still others are one-time tasks to do once, then check on from time to time.

But some others are complex responses to danger that need dedicated and focused rehearsal until you can do them even when you're compromised. As adults, we should practice them until we can do everything successfully while drunk. For kids, they should practice until you can see them do it without hesitation or pause.

The best recommendation I've heard on this is to make safety drills part of your monthly family calendar. Choose a different one each month and practice together. As your children get older, you can put them in charge sometimes to add another level of consideration and responsibility.

It works even better if you create plans that use intersecting skills and knowledge. Your fire plan and your home intruder plan might be the same: everybody get out and convene at the neighbor's house. All of your bug-out scenarios begin with grabbing equipment and heading for the car. First aid for any number of injuries starts with the same basic steps, including calling for help.

Setting up rehearsals and drills that apply the same skills doesn't just reinforce your family's responses to different threats. It builds competence in basic safety disciplines. Competence breeds confidence, and confidence can help slow and reduce the stress reactions that stop us from thinking clearly when it matters most.

Building Habits One at a Time. When I say to practice the hundred habits before this one in the book, I don't mean to take them all on at once. If you try to take them all on, you'll end up overwhelmed and frustrated, and end up with little to no progress.

Instead, I recommend choosing just one habit to focus on for one quarter. Build the habit slowly, with your family, with some kind of focus once or twice a week. At the end of three months, you will be better at it than most other adults. It doesn't take much of an evolution to become skilled enough to be much safer.

At the end of that quarter, choose another habit and focus on it. Before long, you will have developed all the skills you need, and so will have your kids.

Four Stages of Competence. Psychologist and management trainer Martin W. Broadwell first put this model forward. Like all models, it's not a perfect match for reality, but it's been a useful framework for me when teaching safety skills and managing expectations about progress.

Broadwell identified four stages of competence for any set of skills or knowledge. Those stages are:

- **Unconscious Incompetence**: You're doing something wrong and don't know enough to even realize you're doing it wrong.
- **Conscious Incompetence**: You know enough to see your mistakes but not enough to reliably avoid those mistakes.

- **Conscious Competence**: With focus you can do it right and realize you are doing it right.
- **Unconscious Competence**: You do it right without conscious thought and effort. The skill has become reflexive.

It's easiest to envision this with a physical skill like throwing a ball at a target. You start flailing, not sure which parts of your stance or arm motion are making a difference. Next, you know sometimes when a throw is going to miss but you're not sure how you know. In the next stage, you're hitting the target regularly when you're on your game. Finally, you can always hit the target even when you're really focusing on something else.

Applied to practicing safety skills and plans, this model can help you assess your family's preparedness and level of training.

Keep in mind, though: this is not a linear progression. Although it's more or less chronological, you know from your own learning experiences that there's an ebb and flow to it. You make forward progress, then backslide, then move forward, then plateau.

All of this is normal and natural. Do your best to avoid using it as a tool for getting frustrated about your progress toward safety. Instead, use it as a measuring stick. Your tape measure doesn't judge or despair over how long lumber is.

Why Training Matters. I'll close this with another safety quote from a different Special Forces operator. I hadn't heard it before, but I gather it's a truism among people in that field.

We don't rise to the occasion.
We fall to our level of training.

Let's commit to training our families in the ways they can keep themselves and each other safe. Practice that training and watch everybody rise.

ABOUT THE AUTHOR

Jason Brick has been a martial artist for thirty-nine years, a journalist for fifteen, and a father for sixteen. He hosts the *Safest Family on the Block* podcast and speaks internationally on the topics of parenting, martial arts, and safety. His work has appeared in venues that include *Black Belt* magazine, Insider, Thrillist, *Your Teen Mag*, Healthline, *Martial Journal*, and *Inside Kung Fu*. His book on violence prevention, *There I Was When Nothing Happened*, is an international best seller, and he is also the coauthor of the forthcoming book *Verbal Judo's Five Universal Truths of Human Interaction*.

Jason's non-writing, non-martial-arts hobbies include tabletop role-playing games, travel, cooking, and spoiling his wife and sons. He lives in Oregon with his family and three cats.

BOOKS FROM YMAA

101 REFLECTIONS ON TAI CHI CHUAN
108 INSIGHTS INTO TAI CHI CHUAN
A WOMAN'S QIGONG GUIDE
ADVANCING IN TAE KWON DO
ANALYSIS OF GENUINE KARATE
ANALYSIS OF GENUINE KARATE 2
ANALYSIS OF SHU HA RI IN KARATE-DO
ANALYSIS OF SHAOLIN CHIN NA 2ND ED
ANCIENT CHINESE WEAPONS
ART AND SCIENCE OF STAFF FIGHTING
THE ART AND SCIENCE OF SELF-DEFENSE
ART AND SCIENCE OF STICK FIGHTING
ART OF HOJO UNDO
ARTHRITIS RELIEF
BACK PAIN RELIEF
BAGUAZHANG
BRAIN FITNESS
CHIN NA IN GROUND FIGHTING
CHINESE FAST WRESTLING
CHINESE FITNESS
CHINESE TUI NA MASSAGE
COMPLETE MARTIAL ARTIST
COMPREHENSIVE APPLICATIONS OF SHAOLIN CHIN NA
CONFLICT COMMUNICATION
DAO DE JING: A QIGONG INTERPRETATION
DAO IN ACTION
DEFENSIVE TACTICS
DIRTY GROUND
DR. WU'S HEAD MASSAGE
ESSENCE OF SHAOLIN WHITE CRANE
EXPLORING TAI CHI
FACING VIOLENCE
FIGHT LIKE A PHYSICIST
THE FIGHTER'S BODY
FIGHTER'S FACT BOOK 1&2
FIGHTING THE PAIN RESISTANT ATTACKER
FIRST DEFENSE
FORCE DECISIONS: A CITIZENS GUIDE
HOMECOMING
INSIDE TAI CHI
JUDO ADVANTAGE
JUJI GATAME ENCYCLOPEDIA
KARATE SCIENCE
KEPPAN
KRAV MAGA COMBATIVES
KRAV MAGA FUNDAMENTAL STRATEGIES
KRAV MAGA PROFESSIONAL TACTICS
KRAV MAGA WEAPON DEFENSES
LITTLE BLACK BOOK OF VIOLENCE
LIUHEBAFA FIVE CHARACTER SECRETS
MARTIAL ARTS OF VIETNAM
MARTIAL ARTS INSTRUCTION
MARTIAL WAY AND ITS VIRTUES
MEDITATIONS ON VIOLENCE
MERIDIAN QIGONG EXERCISES
MINDFUL EXERCISE
MIND INSIDE TAI CHI
MIND INSIDE YANG STYLE TAI CHI CHUAN
NORTHERN SHAOLIN SWORD
OKINAWA'S COMPLETE KARATE SYSTEM: ISSHIN RYU
PRINCIPLES OF TRADITIONAL CHINESE MEDICINE
PROTECTOR ETHIC
QIGONG FOR HEALTH & MARTIAL ARTS
QIGONG FOR TREATING COMMON AILMENTS

QIGONG MASSAGE
QIGONG MEDITATION: EMBRYONIC BREATHING
QIGONG GRAND CIRCULATION
QIGONG MEDITATION: SMALL CIRCULATION
QIGONG, THE SECRET OF YOUTH: DA MO'S CLASSICS
ROOT OF CHINESE QIGONG
SAFEST FAMILY ON THE BLOCK
SAMBO ENCYCLOPEDIA
SCALING FORCE
SELF-DEFENSE FOR WOMEN
SHIN GI TAI: KARATE TRAINING
SIMPLE CHINESE MEDICINE
SIMPLE QIGONG EXERCISES FOR HEALTH, 3RD ED.
SIMPLIFIED TAI CHI CHUAN, 2ND ED.
SOLO TRAINING 1&2
SPOTTING DANGER BEFORE IT SPOTS YOU
SPOTTING DANGER BEFORE IT SPOTS YOUR KIDS
SPOTTING DANGER BEFORE IT SPOTS YOUR TEENS
SPOTTING DANGER FOR TRAVELERS
SUMO FOR MIXED MARTIAL ARTS
SUNRISE TAI CHI
SURVIVING ARMED ASSAULTS
TAE KWON DO: THE KOREAN MARTIAL ART
TAEKWONDO BLACK BELT POOMSAE
TAEKWONDO: A PATH TO EXCELLENCE
TAEKWONDO: ANCIENT WISDOM
TAEKWONDO: DEFENSE AGAINST WEAPONS
TAEKWONDO: SPIRIT AND PRACTICE
TAI CHI BALL QIGONG: FOR HEALTH AND MARTIAL ARTS
TAI CHI BALL QIGONG
THE TAI CHI BOOK
TAI CHI CHIN NA
TAI CHI CHUAN CLASSICAL YANG STYLE
TAI CHI CHUAN MARTIAL APPLICATIONS
TAI CHI CHUAN MARTIAL POWER
TAI CHI CONCEPTS AND EXPERIMENTS
TAI CHI DYNAMICS
TAI CHI FOR DEPRESSION
TAI CHI IN 10 WEEKS
TAI CHI PUSH HANDS
TAI CHI QIGONG
TAI CHI SECRETS OF THE ANCIENT MASTERS
TAI CHI SECRETS OF THE WU & LI STYLES
TAI CHI SECRETS OF THE WU STYLE
TAI CHI SECRETS OF THE YANG STYLE
TAI CHI SWORD: CLASSICAL YANG STYLE
TAI CHI SWORD FOR BEGINNERS
TAI CHI WALKING
TAI CHI CHUAN THEORY OF DR. YANG, JWING-MING
FIGHTING ARTS
TRADITIONAL CHINESE HEALTH SECRETS
TRADITIONAL TAEKWONDO
TRAINING FOR SUDDEN VIOLENCE
TRIANGLE HOLD ENCYCLOPEDIA
TRUE WELLNESS SERIES (MIND, HEART, GUT)
WARRIOR'S MANIFESTO
WAY OF KATA
WAY OF SANCHIN KATA
WAY TO BLACK BELT
WESTERN HERBS FOR MARTIAL ARTISTS
WILD GOOSE QIGONG
WING CHUN IN-DEPTH
WINNING FIGHTS
XINGYIQUAN

AND MANY MORE . . .

VIDEOS FROM YMAA

ANALYSIS OF SHAOLIN CHIN NA
ART AND SCIENCE OF SELF DEFENSE
ART AND SCIENCE OF STAFF FIGHTING
ART AND SCIENCE STICK FIGHTING
ART AND SCIENCE SWORD FIGHTING
BAGUA FOR BEGINNERS 1 & 2
BEGINNER QIGONG FOR WOMEN 1 & 2
BEGINNER TAI CHI FOR HEALTH
BREATH MEDICINE
BIOENERGY TRAINING 1&2
CHEN TAI CHI CANNON FIST
CHEN TAI CHI FIRST FORM
CHEN TAI CHI FOR BEGINNERS
CHIN NA IN-DEPTH SERIES
FACING VIOLENCE: 7 THINGS A MARTIAL ARTIST MUST KNOW
FIVE ANIMAL SPORTS
FIVE ELEMENTS ENERGY BALANCE
HEALER WITHIN: MEDICAL QIGONG
INFIGHTING
INTRODUCTION TO QI GONG FOR BEGINNERS
JOINT LOCKS
KUNG FU BODY CONDITIONING 1 & 2
KUNG FU FOR KIDS AND TEENS SERIES
MERIDIAN QIGONG
NEIGONG FOR MARTIAL ARTS
NORTHERN SHAOLIN SWORD
QI GONG 30-DAY CHALLENGE
QI GONG FOR ANXIETY
QI GONG FOR ARMS, WRISTS, AND HANDS
QIGONG FOR BEGINNERS: FRAGRANCE
QI GONG FOR BETTER BALANCE
QI GONG FOR BETTER BREATHING
QI GONG FOR CANCER
QI GONG FOR DEPRESSION
QI GONG FOR ENERGY AND VITALITY
QI GONG FOR HEADACHES
QIGONG FOR HEALTH: BETTER DIGESTION
QIGONG FOR HEALTH: HEALING QIGONG EXERCISES
QIGONG FOR HEALTH: IMMUNE SYSTEM
QIGONG FOR HEALTH: JOINT REHABILITATION
QIGONG FOR HEALTH: MERIDIAN EXTREMITIES
QIGONG FOR HEALTH: SITTING QIGONG EXERCISES
QIGONG FOR HEALTH: SPINE AND BACK
QI GONG FOR THE HEALTHY HEART
QI GONG FOR HEALTHY JOINTS
QI GONG FOR HIGH BLOOD PRESSURE
QIGONG FOR LONGEVITY
QI GONG FOR STRONG BONES
QI GONG FOR THE UPPER BACK AND NECK
QIGONG FOR WOMEN WITH DAISY LEE
QIGONG FLOW FOR STRESS & ANXIETY RELIEF
QIGONG GRAND CIRCULATION
QIGONG MASSAGE
QIGONG MINDFULNESS IN MOTION
QI GONG—THE SEATED WORKOUT
QIGONG: 15 MINUTES TO HEALTH
SABER FUNDAMENTAL TRAINING
SAI TRAINING AND SEQUENCES
SANCHIN KATA: TRADITIONAL TRAINING FOR KARATE POWER
SCALING FORCE
SEARCHING FOR SUPERHUMANS
SHAOLIN KUNG FU FUNDAMENTAL TRAINING: COURSES 1 & 2
SHAOLIN LONG FIST KUNG FU BEGINNER-INTERMEDIATE-ADVANCED
    SERIES
SHAOLIN SABER: BASIC SEQUENCES
SHAOLIN STAFF: BASIC SEQUENCES
SHAOLIN WHITE CRANE GONG FU BASIC TRAINING SERIES
SHUAI JIAO: KUNG FU WRESTLING
SIMPLE QIGONG EXERCISES FOR HEALTH
SIMPLE QIGONG EXERCISES FOR ARTHRITIS RELIEF

SIMPLE QIGONG EXERCISES FOR BACK PAIN RELIEF
SIMPLIFIED TAI CHI CHUAN: 24 & 48 POSTURES
SIMPLIFIED TAI CHI FOR BEGINNERS 48
SPOTTING DANGER BEFORE IT SPOTS YOU
SPOTTING DANGER FOR KIDS
SPOTTING DANGER FOR TEENS
SUN TAI CHI
SWORD: FUNDAMENTAL TRAINING
TAEKWONDO KORYO POOMSAE
TAI CHI BALL QIGONG SERIES
TAI CHI BALL WORKOUT FOR BEGINNERS
TAI CHI CHUAN CLASSICAL YANG STYLE
TAI CHI FIGHTING SET
TAI CHI FIT: 24 FORM
TAI CHI FIT: ALZHEIMER'S PREVENTION
TAI CHI FIT: CANCER PREVENTION
TAI CHI FIT FOR VETERANS
TAI CHI FIT: FOR WOMEN
TAI CHI FIT: FLOW
TAI CHI FIT: FUSION BAMBOO
TAI CHI FIT: FUSION FIRE
TAI CHI FIT: FUSION IRON
TAI CHI FIT: HEALTHY BACK SEATED WORKOUT
TAI CHI FIT: HEALTHY HEART WORKOUT
TAI CHI FIT IN PARADISE
TAI CHI FIT: OVER 50
TAI CHI FIT OVER 50: BALANCE EXERCISES
TAI CHI FIT OVER 50: SEATED WORKOUT
TAI CHI FIT OVER 60: GENTLE EXERCISES
TAI CHI FIT OVER 60: HEALTHY JOINTS
TAI CHI FIT OVER 60: LIVE LONGER
TAI CHI FIT: STRENGTH
TAI CHI FIT: TO GO
TAI CHI FOR WOMEN
TAI CHI FUSION: FIRE
TAI CHI QIGONG
TAI CHI PRINCIPLES FOR HEALTHY AGING
TAI CHI PUSHING HANDS SERIES
TAI CHI SWORD: CLASSICAL YANG STYLE
TAI CHI SWORD FOR BEGINNERS
TAI CHI SYMBOL: YIN YANG STICKING HANDS
TAIJI & SHAOLIN STAFF: FUNDAMENTAL TRAINING
TAIJI CHIN NA IN-DEPTH
TAIJI 37 POSTURES MARTIAL APPLICATIONS
TAIJI SABER CLASSICAL YANG STYLE
TAIJI WRESTLING
TRAINING FOR SUDDEN VIOLENCE
UNDERSTANDING QIGONG SERIES
WHITE CRANE HARD & SOFT QIGONG
YANG TAI CHI FOR BEGINNERS
YOQI: MICROCOSMIC ORBIT QIGONG
YOQI QIGONG FOR A HAPPY HEART
YOQI:QIGONG FLOW FOR HAPPY MIND
YOQI:QIGONG FLOW FOR INTERNAL ALCHEMY
YOQI QIGONG FOR HAPPY SPLEEN & STOMACH
YOQI QIGONG FOR HAPPY KIDNEYS
YOQI QIGONG FLOW FOR HAPPY LUNGS
YOQI QIGONG FLOW FOR STRESS RELIEF
YOQI: QIGONG FLOW TO BOOST IMMUNE SYSTEM
YOQI SIX HEALING SOUNDS
YOQI: YIN YOGA 1
WU TAI CHI FOR BEGINNERS
WUDANG KUNG FU: FUNDAMENTAL TRAINING
WUDANG SWORD
WUDANG TAIJIQUAN
XINGYIQUAN
YANG TAI CHI FOR BEGINNERS

AND MANY MORE . . .

more products available from . . .

YMAA Publication Center, Inc. 楊氏東方文化出版中心

1-800-669-8892 • info@ymaa.com • www.ymaa.com